A Lifetime of Joy

A collection of circle games, finger games, songs, verses, and plays for puppets and marionettes

Collected, created, adapted, and translated by Bronja Zahlingen of the Rudolf Steiner Kindergarten Vienna, Austria

Editorial Committee: Susan Howard, Barbara Klocek and Stephen Spitalny
Managing Editor: Lydia Roberson
Design and Illustration: Sheila Harrington, Studio Five
Music: Nancy Foster
Text Editing: Sandy Milczarek and Lydia Roberson
Administrative Support: Melissa Lyons

Special thanks to Joan Almon and Brigitte Goldmann.

© Waldorf Early Childhood Association of North America

First Edition, 2005

Published in the United States by the
Waldorf Early Childhood Association of North America
285 Hungry Hollow Road
Spring Valley, NY 10977

Library of Congress Cataloging-in-Publication Data
0-9722238-6-X

10 9 8 7 6 5 4 3 2 1

All rights reserved. No part of this book may be reproduced in any form without the written permission of the publisher, except for brief quotations embodied in critical reviews and articles.

This book is made possible by a grant from the Waldorf Curriculum Fund.

Table of Contents

Bronja Zahlingen iii
Publisher's Note vii
Introduction to First Edition ix
In Praise of Early Childhood 1
Movement, Gesture, and Language in the Life of the Young Child 5
The Pedagogical Value of Marionette
and Table Puppet Shows for the Small Child 11

Verses and Songs 15
    Pitter Patter 15
    The Busy Bee 15
    Butter Churn 15
    My Ma 16
    Riding Horse 16
    Rocking Boat Song 16
    Fish Game 16
    Tip a Tap 16
    Violets 17
    Snowdrops 17
    Snow 17
    The Hazelmouse 18
    The Shepherd Boy 18

Circle Games 19
    Autumn Circle 19
    Spring Circle 23
    Foxglove: A Circle Game for Midsummer 25
    Birthday Game 28

Stories 29
    Little Grandmother Evergreen 29
    A Garden Full of Wonder 30
    The Blue Caterpillar 30
    Little Flea and Little Louse 32

    The Little Madam 33

    The Little Castle 34

    Atty-Atty-Attic 36

    The Mitten 37

Plays for Puppets and Marionettes 39

    The Giant and the Gnome 39

    The Hungry Cat 39

    Cat and Mouse 42

    The Mushroom in the Rain 43

    The Little Boy Who Wanted To Be Carried Along All the Time 45

    The Little Light Horse 47

    Little Spring Play 52

    A Summer Play for Small Marionettes 55

    Mashenka and the Bear 60

    The Swan Geese 64

    The Snowmaiden 66

    Goldener 70

    The Queen Bee 75

    Twiggy 79

    The Miller Boy and the Pussycat 82

    A Midsummer Tale 88

    The Three Oranges 93

    Play of the Four Seasons 97

    Directions for Simple Marionettes 105

Nature Tales and Christmas Legends 107

    The Turtle, the Spider and the Wagtail 107

    How Thyme Became So Sweet Smelling 107

    The Shepherd in the Feather Bed 108

    The Christmas Rose 108

    How the Daisies Came into the World 109

    Vineling, Morning Glory 109

    Mary's Journey Over the Stars: A Story for Advent Garden 109

    St. Nicholas 110

Footnotes 111

Sources 113

Cultivated humanity is a blessing for the world.
—Pestalozzi

Bronja Zahlingen
January 8, 1912–January 24, 2000

Bronja Zahlingen's life was devoted to the care of little children. "They need a nourishing, healthy breakfast to last them for their whole journey through life," was the way she expressed it. She devoted herself to preparing this "breakfast" for over sixty years.

Tiny and delicate in stature, she also was filled with a very strong will that clearly affected the course of her life and work. Bronja was born as Bronja Huettner, the youngest child of a Jewish family on a country estate in Poland; they had to leave Poland at the outbreak of World War I and came to live in Vienna. As a high school student in the Wasa-Gymnasium, Bronja first encountered anthroposophy through her classmates Rudi Lissau and Hans Schauder and others. Her future husband also belonged to this circle of friends. After discovering that university studies in psychology were not suited for her, she began a kindergarten training.

In 1932, as a twenty-year-old, she joined the Anthroposophical Society and began to build up a kindergarten in Vienna; soon it was brimming with life. This activity, along with the development of the Waldorf School and the Anthroposophical Society, came to an abrupt end with the invasion of Hitler's troops in 1938.

Bronja's visit to a conference in England led to an extended stay, and thus she avoided the terrible fate of her mother and sister in Theresienstadt—only her brother survived. Her emigration lasted eleven years. She was able to teach German and classical languages and help in the

> "Where are the snowdrops?"
> asked the Sun.
> "Dead" said the Frost
> "buried and lost, every one"
> "O no!" said the Sun
> "They did not die,
> asleep they lie
> and I will wake them, I
> Up to the light
> all dressed in white,
> every one!"

Handwritten verses by Bronja Zahlingen

> Pitter, patter, pitter patter
> look at all the rain
> knocking on the window sill
> and on the window pane.
> Sounding like the pitter pat
> of little fairy feet
> running down the garden path,
> running down the street.
> Washing every body's house
> and every body's shop,
> Pitter patter, pitter patter
> when is it going to stop?!

kindergarten at Michael Hall, a Waldorf school in Sussex, until she was sent, along with many other refugees, to an internment camp on the Isle of Man. During this extremely difficult period, her physical health was weakened—many of her later health problems had their origins here—but her inner forces and commitment to her future path grew stronger.

After ten years of separation, she was reunited with her friend from earlier years, Hans Zahlingen; their friendship was rekindled and they married in England in 1949. Bronja would have liked to remain in England, but her husband's work took them back to Vienna, where their only child, a son, was born in 1950.

Bronja became a leading figure in the efforts to found a Waldorf kindergarten in Vienna. By 1955 it was finally possible for her to begin working in a kindergarten in the Third Precinct, taking her own little son along. After several changes in location, the kindergarten—together with the Zahlingen family—finally found its home on Reisner Strasse.

Once the school had seven grades and moved into its own facilities at the Maurer Castle ground, plans were undertaken for a kindergarten near the school. The building of the kindergarten was financed through large and small gifts, including the proceeds from the sale of a small Breughel painting and permission from the city to build on lands set aside for agricultural use. In 1972, the foundation stone was laid, with Dr. Helmut von Kuegelgen in attendance, and the following year the new kindergarten was opened. This was a high point in Bronja's career, overshadowed though by the death of her husband.

Bronja had been involved from the very beginning with the founding of the school in Vienna, and now lived and worked in close connection with the school, where she also taught religious instruction classes and offered the Sunday services for children.

Bronja led a kindergarten group until 1980. Many colleagues were able to participate in the School for the Art of Education there, and to experience Bronja as a model and example. Her linguistic creations—verses and rhythmic games, poems and stories—poured into the daily life of the kindergarten, along with puppetry and marionette plays, both poetic and light-hearted, which were created from the simplest materials. Perhaps its was this very simplicity and authenticity that so enchanted the children and also the parents, who were thus guided into the realm of the imagination, of fantasy. Through her light touch, many wool picture creations were hung on the walls and many, many generations of puppets of all sizes—angels and animals, dwarves and elves, and the figures of the nativity story—were created. They all found their place of honor at the Advent fairs, increasingly augmented by the creations of parents and helpers who attended her puppet-making classes.

Perhaps, however, it belongs to the destiny of all pioneer figures—and Bronja Zahlingen was truly such a pioneer in her work after World War II—that they do not always make it easy for their colleagues and successors, despite the recognition of their talents and capacities, to develop their own ways and styles of working. But the fullness of suggestions and impulses for the development of the work, out of her deep understanding for the being of the little child, could always stimulate enthusiasm and build bridges in personal encounters and conversation.

In the final phase of Bronja's working life, she turned her attention to the developing kindergarten movement in the United States, through courses and consulting work, and her connection to those in the English-speaking world and to the English language itself remained very strong and active. Her little verses and stories were able to be published in German and in English. (See Publisher's Note on page vii.)

Bronja was an active participant in the development of the International Waldorf Kindergarten Association. She began attending international conferences in 1957/58 in Hanover, Germany, and until 1990 she was a member of the board of the International Association. Global awarenss and Waldorf education for all children of this world were always of great concern to her.

The decline of her delicate and sensitive physical being led to the end of her active working life; however, since she lived in the same building as the kindergarten, she continued to be able to participate in the many festivals that were celebrated there. In 1997, her weakened condition required more constant care, and Bronja found loving attentiveness and care at a social therapeutic village community called Breitenfurt for the final three years of her life.

Creating a space for children in which their future humanity could develop—this was the life task to which Bronja Zahlingen devoted herself, out of the wellsprings of her ability to find the child within herself throughout her whole long life. We have learned much from her.

Brigitte Goldman and Elisabeth Gergeley
Vienna

Publisher's Note

Joan Almon of the Acorn Hill Children's Center in Maryland spent a year in Vienna while her husband was on sabbatical there in the late 1970's, and it was there that Joan encountered Bronja's work. A rich colleagueship and friendship developed, and Bronja became a frequent visitor to the United States, first to Acorn Hill and then as an annual visiting faculty member at the Waldorf Institute/Sunbridge College.

Bronja taught courses in Language Arts and Puppetry for the Young Child there for nearly ten years. She visited kindergartens and offered many puppetry workshops, also at Rudolf Steiner College, at the Rudolf Steiner Institute in Maine, and at the first North American Waldorf Kindergarten Conference in 1989 in Wilton, NH. Her first collection of *Plays for Puppets* was published by Acorn Hill; it includes "Mashenka and the Bear," "The Snowmaiden," and "Swan Geese," which are now among the most beloved puppet plays experienced by a generation of North American Waldorf kindergarten children. Now, twenty years later, we extend the first volume to include a wider collection of Bronja's creations and writings. Understanding, warmth, joy and enthusiasm are needed today more than ever by those who care for young children, and the enkindling of the imagination, to which Bronja devoted herself, becomes an urgent need for the children in our care.

Susan Howard

Introduction to First Edition

The first edition of this booklet contained only plays for puppets and marionettes. As we create this new edition, we recognize Bronja Zahlingen's lifelong commitment to young children. We have enlarged her original booklet to include additional plays, but also her articles that appeared in past issues of the Waldorf Kindergarten Newsletter. We also include songs and verses much loved in her Vienna Kindergarten and translated by her long-time colleague, Brigitte Goldmann, for use by English-speaking teachers.

For many years, I visited and worked in the United States with students and teachers of Waldorf education concerning the needs of the young child. At their request I offer the following collection of rhymes and stories for puppet plays that I have now translated and presented up to now. Some of these stories we have already performed together.

The rhymes and stories are meant for the enjoyment and benefit of children up to the age of about nine years and can serve as a working impulse and starting point for those concerned with child guidance. They can be enacted with standing figures, knotted dolls, string puppets or simple marionettes. Hand puppets are also possible, but then a different arrangement for the setting is necessary.

Puppetry scenery is best built up with silks, cottons, and natural materials such as bits of bark, wood, shells, and stones, which are spread on the tables or on the floor. Where a background is necessary, silks and cottons will shine and drape best. The right colors will create the right mood. The whole scene is unveiled carefully while the children watch with great expectation and with feelings of wonder and surprise.

The performing adult may be seen as she handles the puppets and tells the story. (You can also have a special storyteller, as well as someone to help with the music.) Seeing the performer does not disturb the young child at all—he soon forgets, as he is interested in what is happening. His inner experience is strengthened, because he sees that in order for things to happen some person must be the moving force. The fact is that, through technical perfection, actions in our time tend to become automatic and anonymous, which is apt to diminish the feeling of individual responsibility and to create a false understanding of the world. Such an attitude taken from childhood into adult life can hold grave dangers that reach up into the level of morality.

It is also important for the right development and activity of the child's senses that he can watch such a play take place in actual space—length, breadth and depth; otherwise, his sense organs are easily stupefied and made passive. If the child can see the stories unfold step by step, grow and change in the simple but beautiful way described, the pictures can be taken right into the stream of his life forces, without creating hard and fixed impressions. Pictures of action which appear to be moving on a flat screen, brought about artificially by technical skill, confuse the young child's eye, his sense of direction and movement, and often even his mind. Such an experience could easily become worrying and depressing, leaving the child a helpless onlooker standing outside the creative process he is viewing.

The simplicity and transparency of our table plays call forth the child's power of imagination, and she is right in the midst of all that takes place. Through this, the creative power for her own play, as well as for her own movement and language development, are stimulated. In this way the child can also be helped to become a person of independence and creative activity in later life.

I have to thank many friends for either a story or music, for helping with the typing, corrections, etc. We are all indebted to and inspired by the work of Rudolf Steiner, through which our own endeavors can acquire the understanding, the warmth and enthusiasm that are so much needed in the service of the children today.

Bronja Zahlingen
Vienna, March 1982

*Little children grow and flourish
By the loving care we give;
Our smiles and gentle kindness
In their very hearts can live.*

*Guardian angel takes the treasure,
Carries it to heights above;
Tending like a little seedling,
Sweet remembrance of our love.*

*In the start-lit realms of heaven,
Keeping it in God's own light,
'Til again He, earthward bending,
Back to us does wing his flight.*

*Bearing in His hands of silver
Blessing to the earth below
Lo, behold the change and wonder,
Roses in our garden grow.*

—Bronja Zahlingen

In Praise of Early Childhood

What a privilege it is to be concerned with children during the first years of their lives, to witness the gradual shaping of their features and expressions; to perceive how their movements and gestures begin to individualize that universal gift bestowed upon us all: the "Human Form Divine," as William Blake called it. Innocence still weaves a transparent shining quality around the heads of these little ones—their very presence awakens reverence in the soul, and a feeling of wonder at the incarnation process of the individual.

Little children seem to be in the laps of the gods for their first two-and-a-half years, during which they achieve those essential human faculties: the upright walk, the power of articulate speech, and the first shaping of thought. Only then does the feeling of being an ego arise. These are gifts of a creative world higher than ours: they well up from the inmost core of the child, revealing will activity from within. In this entire process we can only be helpers. While the physical organs and their functions are being thus structured, we can glimpse how the individuality struggles between the two contributions of the physical world: between heredity on the one hand and environment on the other. Yet it is that unique entity's task at this early age, to shape and transform these two influences to the best possible degree in order to create a more or less suitable instrument to serve the personality's own free way of dealing with life and destiny later on.

Human beings can change and develop beyond their natural genetic and biological dispositions, on which their spiritual, soul and moral qualities never entirely depend. Here we begin to understand the great responsibility that rests upon us adults, as parents and educators; in fact, upon the whole attitude and environment that a particular place, culture or civilization has to offer.

In the presence of young children, this responsibility is especially great because in their earliest years, children are endowed with an immense power of imitation that can also reveal the great trust and confidence they have in us and in the world around them. They cannot yet distinguish values, and seem to assume that everything around them is good. During this period of life, body, soul and spirit still exist as a unity.

Children's pleasure and displeasure are visible right down to the tips of their toes; they can seem to be twice their normal weight if they do not wish to be moved. While thus engaged in building and developing their bodies, children form tendencies toward good or ill health, depending on their physical and soul experiences. The very functions of their organs are influenced by the warmth and friendliness we offer, even by our inner striving and moral intentions. Somehow, little children seem to see right through us.

If we take seriously the fact that efficiently-functioning sense organs are established at this period of life, the need will be obvious to give full play to finer differentiations of the eye, the ear, the sense of touch and all of the other channels through which we perceive the world around us. If we overstrain the senses too early through mechanical and technological experiences, they will of necessity harden and deteriorate prematurely, and will then be unfit for more intimate and varied perception. This can even have serious social consequences.

Therefore, we must surround young children with the genuine quality of natural materials, such as cotton, silk, wood or stone; we must have clear, beautiful colors around them, spoken language, music directly through song or suitable instruments, and good honest playthings.

The play of children from the age of three is a most wonderful thing to watch. They will build up a little world of their own and be sovereigns in it. They can put a piece of wood in an upright position—thereby giving it the semblance of a person—or use a cooking spoon, which then must be wrapped up in pieces of cloth, for a doll. Even a knotted handkerchief will come alive and take on all kinds of shapes and forms in this gradually arising ability of imaginative play. But the child's mind and intelligence can also be confined in narrow one-track channels by too early intellectual information and explanation, and by most of the so-called teaching toys, which disregard the universal scope of the unfolding spirit at play, with which the unspoiled child is naturally blessed. I would like to quote William Blake with the following lines from his *Songs of Innocence*[1]:

To see a World in a Grain of Sand
And a Heaven in a Wild Flower,
Hold Infinity in the palm of your hand
And Eternity in an hour.

Here lies one of the essential roots of the creativity for which everyone craves today. This free imaginative play undergoes many stages of varied development in the preschool years, which through the knowledge of the human being given by Rudolf Steiner, we learn ever better to understand.

With the advent of the second dentition, the living formative forces are released to some extent from their shaping, molding activities within the physical body, and appear also as artistic abilities, so necessary for true learning; they lead into a much wider field of fantasy with the help of the soul forces that are more strongly at work during the grade school years, and can eventually become living, constructive thought.

Our world will depend more and more on the creative spirit of the individual, who must emerge as an adaptable and open-minded person with social and moral initiative. This can never be achieved by demands or admonitions; it must grow and develop through all the stages of education and self-education. The foundations are laid and nurtured in the early years of childhood if the children experience love and joy and goodness in their environment. If their power of imitation is given plenty of scope through meeting mature and active people doing constructive work and service, then their experiences can be freely taken over into the individual creative activity of play and artistic expression. By preserving something of the childlike qualities and forces for later life, as well as by experiencing all that we must undergo in life in order to become free and responsible men and women, we may well be helped to find answers to the urgent needs of our time.

So we will close with another excerpt from William Blake's *Songs of Innocence*[2] to bring home to ourselves the quality of early childhood:

Little Lamb, who made thee?
Dost thou know who made thee?
Gave thee life, and bid thee feed,
By the stream and o'er the mead;
Gave thee clothing of delight,
Softest clothing, wooly, bright;
Gave thee such a tender voice,
Making all the vales rejoice;
Little Lamb, who made thee?
Dost thou know who made thee?
Little Lamb, I'll tell thee,
Little Lamb, I'll tell thee:
He is called by thy name,
For He calls himself a Lamb.
He is meek, and He is mild;
He became a little child.
I, a child, and thou a lamb,
We are called by His name.
Little Lamb, God bless thee!
Little Lamb, God bless thee!

Movement, Gesture, and Language in the Life of a Young Child

We are filled with respect and wonder when we consider how each and every human individual, after coming from the spiritual world, is able to feel so at home with life on earth in the very earliest years. It is through the three important stages of becoming—walking, speaking and learning to think—that each child opens herself up to the conditions of her physical, soul and objective spiritual environment. It is like waves breaking on the shore, the constant interplay of the ebb and flow at the ocean's edge. The entire development of the earth is experienced again with the changing phases of metamorphosis.

After accomplishing these steps, the approximately three-year old child can sense and name herself as "I." The human child, crown of creation, who raises herself above the realms of nature by means of these abilities, does so, in order to work with and to feel a loving attachment towards these realms. The child learns to entrust herself to the earth's gravity and its substances, and she learns to overcome it actively through her own higher strengths if we kindly help out by offering our example and protection. Her stirring will wants to go in all directions. She wants to stand upright, to keep her balance between above and below and to walk. She wants to become one with the elements by running, jumping, hopping and sliding. She wants to turn and spin and dance around only to come to rest again and again on good Mother Earth. Children have just such an experience in the old dance meant for the youngest ones:

Ring around the rosies
A pocket full of posies.
A tissue, a tissue
We all fall down.

Right away they do it again and again and again. Children also love to run away, far away, then finally, tired out, they turn around and joyfully rush back into mother's protective arms. Or the child falls down. She would like to cry, but she stretches upwards again, like the little daisies in the meadow. After a heavy rain, the daisies are flattened but with the first ray of sun, they raise their heads toward the light. Hence the custom for English mothers to say, "Up a daisy" if their children trip or fall, and upon hearing it, each child stands gladly up again.

And then there is rocking—first gently in the cradle, half dreaming with soft songs, like being carried along the waves of life's water. Then this motion becomes stronger when they are riding on a knee:

This is the way the ladies ride,
Nimble, nimble, nimble, nimble;
This is the way the gentlemen ride,
A-gallop, a-trot, a-gallop, a-trot;
This is the way the farmers ride,
Jiggety-jog, jiggety-jog;
And when they come to a hedge, they jump over!
And when they come to a slippery place,
They scramble, scramble, scramble,
Tumble-down Dick!

When children are a bit older, the rocking motion is there in their swinging which grows ever more courageous, up and down between heaven and earth. There are truly splendid, lively movements natural to children's games in which the ability to be upright and move rhythmically help to overcome the burden of gravity. "I am so heavy when I sit," said a young schoolboy, joining in an adult conversation about body weight. Children certainly can word their thoughts in such a precise and wonderful way.

The way each child moves—the solidity or inconsistency, the hesitancy or surety of her steps—reveal much about the nature of her will. Recognizing this, we can help to balance and harmonize the child. Once the child has attained the upright position and can keep her balance, her arms and hands become freer and can better grasp the world about her in various ways. This is truly unique to the human being, for the animal, still bound to its physical organization, must utilize its front limbs entirely to serve its body—they must carry and nourish it. We human beings can perform many different kinds of work. We can work with our hands as artists, we can wave and threaten, give and take, pray and bless.

With her arms and hands, the child thus gains a new area of expression—that of the self, an inner, more soul-like quality of expression can be revealed in the "gesture." Archetypal gestures like expansion and contraction, opening and closing into width and narrowness, and tightening and loosening are fundamental gestures in life that are carried out either quickly or slowly, gently or powerfully. The true human gestures of work and all visible activities have been found in children's games as well as the gesture of things in their surroundings, which have taken on a permanent form. These are imitated as well in the soul and growth forces, thus having a strengthening or destructive effect. Gesture precedes the development of language. Indeed, it goes hand in hand with the formation of the speech center in the brain. This also develops in correspondence with the use of the right or left hand. Such gestures as pushing, stooping, touching, grasping and letting go help to develop and form speech sounds. A fluctuation between opening and closing, tightening and loosening develops in conjunction with the rhythm of breathing, and this works on the shaping of the vocal chords and other speech organs. The teeth, lips, tongue, palate and larynx also have a part in this. The outer perception and the inner disposition delicately begin to be formed as soul gesture.

Now, in addition to crying, a child can tell us ever more clearly by the use of words and speech how she feels. When we deepen our study of Rudolf Steiner's rich and varied statements about human speech, its origin and effect, we also become more clearly aware that we unite ourselves with the spiritual in the world through our speech. When speech grows beyond the individual, physical-soul realm, it leads us into a greater, more far-reaching realm, that of the formative creative word. Here we look with deepest gratitude to the essence of eurythmy and its inherent formative and healing power.

The mother tongue is as necessary and nourishing to a child's soul as mother's milk is to her body. The child gradually becomes accustomed to the sound and gesture of the language, its revelations in the rhythm and significance of the word. The child experiences the meaning of a word chiefly in a pictorial manner and not as abstract meaning and concept. For the child it is the diverse, colorful and changing nature of life itself. She takes joy and refreshment in the language when it is abundantly and rhythmically expressed.

There are countless, songs, verses and rhymes for children, both merry and serious, in everyday language and in more poetic form. These are a veritable horn of plenty at the disposal of parents and educators for moderate usage. Here are some examples:

Pick, pack, pull—will the pail soon be full?
Hinka, hanka, hat,
Where is the dog, where is the cat?
The dog is lying near the hearth
Giving himself a nice, clean bath.
The cat is sitting by the window
Licking her fur and each little toe.
 Hinkety, pinkety, heckety, hairs,
The lady is coming up the stairs.
What is she bringing to the kitty?
A ball, a ball, a ball so pretty!
A woolly, white ball in the big house
That looks just like a little mouse.
And to her doggy what does she bring?
 A handsome collar with a golden ring,
A handsome collar of a special kind
With doggy's name in front and behind.
 Hinkety, pinkety, heckety, hout,
Now my tale is all told out.

—Christian Morgenstern

A fingerplay:

Ten little men, see, sitting under the tree.
   The short and the fat are nodding like that.
   The nimble and quick, they dance and they lick.
   The long and the strong come running along.
   The pretty ones sing for a golden ring.
   The babies are tripping and laughing and skipping.
   Be quiet you little ones, lie down and rest,
   Tucked up in your cradle like birds in a nest.

—H. Diestel

An Old English verse:

Round about round about
   In a fair ring-a.
   Thus we dance, thus we dance
   And thus we sing-a
   Trip and go, to and fro,
   Over this green-a
   All about, in and out
   For our brave Queen-a

Or more reflective:

Song of the Sun

I, Mother Sun, hold firm and tight
   the earth by day, the earth by night.
   I hold her fast in my radiant glow,
   so all that lives on her may grow.
   Each man and beast, each plant and tree,
   receive their warming light from me.
   Open your heart, dear child, like a cup
   and let it, too, be lighted up.
   Open your heart, dear child, to the Sun,
   And our two lights will shine as one.[3]

—Christian Morgenstern

Nowadays we slip easily and quickly into the banal and even into the fantastic that is devoid of any inner truth. An example of this is the comic strips that offer children sheer absurdity. They even display what people say as mere air bubbles coming out of their mouths, and these often contain primitive noises (ugh, oof, etc.).

Of course, the Word must at times descend from poetry to the level of prose, but it should at least be meaningful and serve Life. If it remains as mere information, the soul comes out empty-handed, without sympathy for others, in such a way that the social feeling and interest are not aroused.

One poet has already warned us:

"When the soul speaks so, then it is the soul no more."

—Schiller

Moreover, we print many words these days that only serve artificially as empty housing for advertising and profits. At the same time, the words and images of the best poets and painters are becoming distorted and strange, and they stare passersby in the eye from every billboard and kiosk. Fortunately, sometimes a child is still naive and full enough of fantasy to come to his own conclusions, like the first grader who could already read a bit and then asked at home, "Say, Mother, what is a naked wave anyway?" The mother was clearly in a big dilemma about how to answer him when her son solved the whole thing himself by saying, "Ah, I know—it is a wave without foam!"

Our thought life gradually grows into its various forms through the use of language and the formation of words and sentences. It leads step by step to abstraction and conceptualization. But this process is reserved for a later developmental stage (similar to how the whole development of language is accomplished.) But language need not become stiff or hardened—rather it will have to struggle through to new imaginations and higher levels. A conscious, creative and artistic beginning will have to be found, as naiveté is found in the creative, formative language of a child. The child, whose natural inclination is to have his own soul nature conform to that of the adult, needs gestures full of caring affection and helpfulness and a language full of truth. In the tone of the language there also lies a gesture—one can caress with words, as well as explaining and pointing out things. We can loosen what has become hardened and give it new, living form.

The immense impoverishment in the diminishing life forces of nature and especially in the intellectualization of our whole cultural life threatens today's children. Our technical and automated civilization is far removed from the living nature of the small child. The media ruins her senses that need to develop firstly through active use and experience. Direct access to real life, to human gestures, to language and immediate experience of another individuality is falsified and destroyed by the media.

There are many children today who have been damaged in their entire ability to move, for they spend too much time sitting in the car, and they observe and imitate the mechanical running around that takes place on all sides. Thus they walk with stiff, automatic gestures, or they speed about imitating engine noises. There is no time or opportunity to pause, to catch sight of or overhear something more delicate, subtler subtle. Today we find so many basically intelligent, lovable, good-natured children who suddenly, without apparent cause, are seized by fidgeting, jerking and pushing, and who, at times, also seem to explode with strange noises.

Curative attention in movement, gesture and language will become ever more needed as we are able to gain a. deeper, greater insight into the true nature of the human individuality in body, soul and spirit. New creative capabilities will grow in us to replace our lost instincts as well. It is only in this way that we can help to build a suitably human future for and through the children.

The Pedagogical Value of Marionette and Table Puppet Shows for the Small Child

The creative form-giving power of fantasy reveals itself to the careful observer as a soul force, which in the first seven years of life and in many ways even up to the ninth year, appears completely intertwined with the forces of growth. During the development of the wisdom-filled organization of the human body, the flowing streams of life and the shaping, form-giving powers work in a certain polarity. They are unified, however, in unity through the ever working, breathing power of the middle sphere of man.

Tender soul powers are released step-by-step from the life forces and become visible in the child's play, until with the change of teeth, they are ready to be used in the free shaping of concepts. This allows the child to enter school for actual learning that, however, must still be imaginative and full of pictures. At the same time the forces of memory can be guided and used more consciously.

From where, however, does the living fantasy receive its power, the tools for its use? It is the senses that open up the world to the individual being that wants to unfold. In the beginning, they work in unison. The young child appears like one great sense organ which opens itself up to the impressions of the world as a unity of body, soul and spirit; it does not yet consciously decide for one or the other impression, but must in the truest sense of the word "embody" all the impressions which the world makes upon it.

At the birth of a healthy child, the different bodily organs are present with a quality, which fits a human being, but their lasting and individualized shape is formed on the whole during the first seven or even nine years (apart from those organs which begin to ripen in puberty). After that point, soul experiences are mostly working in the functioning rather than the shaping of the organs; growth still continues until the human being comes of age and is in the position of experiencing a soul and spiritual development which is less tied to the body and its organs.

Now let us return to the young child and his senses. (Rudolf Steiner introduces us to the vista of twelve senses in *Knowledge of Higher Worlds*[4], among other places). These senses are gradually differentiated as to their particular quality. They do not, however, like to be completely isolated. The shape of a colored surface, for example, can be understood through inner movement; whatever looks beautiful to the eye is expected to also taste good. The aroma of Christmas cookies will at the same time bring forth in a magical way the memory of the sound of bells, lights on the tree, shining faces, and a sense of true well-being. Through the unity of several senses, the experiences of the soul become richer and more colorful. If the senses act in isolation, the soul is in danger of being impoverished. If, however, through a handicap it becomes necessary to educate the senses in a more isolated way, one will have to give the soul additional experiences in other ways.

Actively, the young child unites with the outer world through his senses. Through the quality of the impressions made on the individual sense organs, he shapes and forms these very organs, making them active and strong, or dull and passive. To come to a better understanding of the development of the senses we can link ourselves to Goethe's words: "The eye is built by the light for the light." If we want the eye to develop the ability of clear sight and sensible perception of colors and forms, we have to guard it in this formative phase of childhood from too strong and glaring experiences of light and color. That which moves and changes too quickly and which the eye has to take in but cannot even follow will possibly create a misforming of the organ of sight."

It is even worse for the ear which we are not able to close voluntarily; here the consequences work even more deeply into the inner being. We understand the consequences brought about by the pleasant qualities in sounds, music and language or by the opposite, namely inorganic, penetrating monotonous noise. A very similar situation exists with the other senses. In our world today only very few children can grow up in the quiet of a garden. Town and countryside are equally flooded by an overflow of sense impressions that change and alter incessantly, and very many children, therefore, have to suffer from outer and inner restlessness.

So as educators we try to create at least some special times for inner quieting, for a deeper breath and concentration. An example of one such opportunity is the play with table puppets or marionettes that children experience at first as observers. Out of this observation, rich impulses can grow for their own play. We build up a scene with pieces of colored cloth, materials taken from nature such as stones, wood, pine cones, unspun wool and such like, and simple home-made standing dolls or animals of wood or soft material. We move the figures in an appropriate way while we tell the story. Or we can create a scene fitting to the content of the story with colored silks or veils. Amidst great expectation, what is mysteriously covered at first is gradually unveiled, and the eye meets a meaningful wholeness. Simple marionettes of silk wander through the colorful world. They walk from house to forest, over the sea and sometimes to sun, moon, and stars, and even sometimes up to the mountain of clear crystal glass. As they move over the surface of the scene using its length, breadth and depth, the observing child can inwardly unite immediately with the experience of space, while on the television only deception of the eye is at work. Here inner activity is created that works in a refreshing and enlivening way into the very breath and blood circulation. Color, movement, gesture and language shape a unity, and fitting music can envelop the soul in warmth and safety. It can also give joy and pleasure.

A little world that is a whole, and which can be fully realized, is given to the child. The child is part of the events because it can share in them through adding, out of its own fantasy, to that which is given to the sense impression as an impulse. For the young children we do not need any technical tricks. The whole event is present as in a picture. As it is happening without a break or an interval, it brings about a pleasing harmony of experience. The other day, after a performance of the story, "The Seven Ravens," a father remarked, "You know, the children become so good." One finds that the adults, too, cannot resist the magic of such a play. The child in us loves to reenter this world of creative imagination that releases a higher vision out of the sense experience.

Last but not least we would point out something rather essential in this kind of puppet play where the person who is leading the dolls remains visible. Not only can we then perceive the reactions of the children and possibly take them into consideration, but also our appearance does not worry the children. Life, body, soul, and spirit still exist as a unity in children. It is only the detachment of the adult that enables us to read the most horrendous reports in the newspaper while at the same time enjoying our lunch; the young child on the contrary, will even eat up food he does not like as he, so to speak, opens himself heart and soul to something nice you are telling him—his open mouth follows! Children's pleasure and displeasure are visible right down to the tips of their toes; they can seem to be twice their normal weight if they do not wish to be moved. While thus engaged in building and developing their bodies, children form tendencies toward good or ill health, depending on their physical and soul experiences. The very functions of their organs are influenced by the warmth and friendliness we offer, even by our inner striving and moral intentions. Somehow, little children seem to see right through us.

Verses and Songs

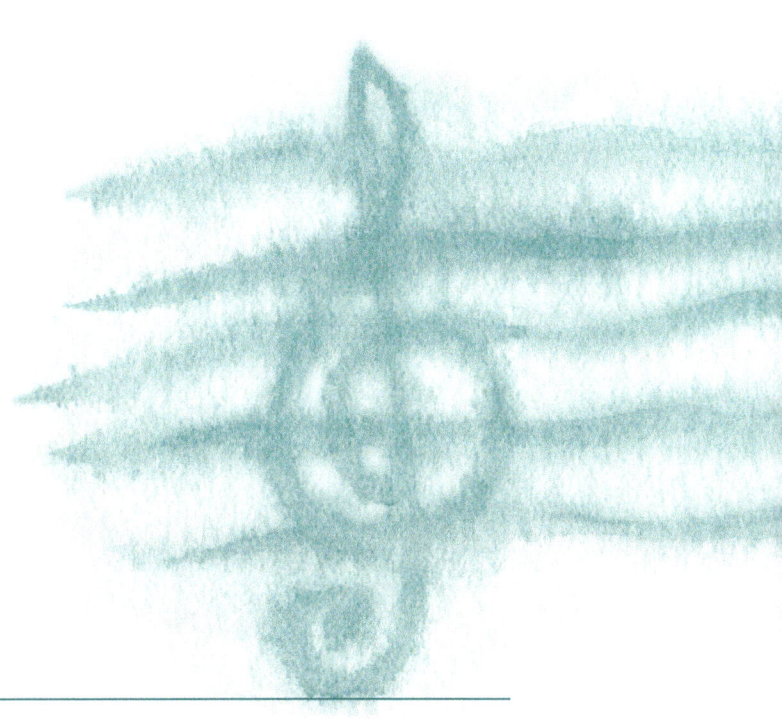

Pitter Patter

Pitter patter, pitter patter,
Look at all the rain,
 Knocking at the windowsill
 And on the windowpane.
 Sounding like the pitter pat of little fairy feet,
 Running down the garden path,
 Running down the street.
 Washing everybody's house and everybody's shop,
 Pitter patter, pitter pat, when is it going to stop?

The Busy Bee

"I'm busy, busy, busy," said the bee.
 "I shan't be home for supper, or for tea.
  It takes me hours and hours to visit all these flowers.
 I'm very, very busy," said the bee.

 "I'm busy, busy, busy," said the bee.
 "I haven't got a single second free.
 It makes me rather dizzy
 And a little wizzy
 To be so very busy," said the bee.

Butter Churn

Rumple Pumple butter churn,
Stir it quickly, give a whirl.

My Ma

My Ma, my Ma, my Mama
sent me on the run,
To fi, to fi, to find out
If it's done.
If no, if no, if not yet all done
I sha, I sha, I shall come soon again.

Riding Horse

Ride along, my rider
Ride along the highway
Ride up to the castle door

Three young maidens stand before
One a-spinning silk-o
One a-weaving yarn-o
The third into the well-go
And find a golden child-o.

Riding rocking horse. Make circle with arms to choose child.

Rocking Boat Song

Roll along my boat
On the waves afloat
Roll along across the sea
Little Johnny comes to me.

Fish Game

I'm catching, catching fish-o
In a little dish-o
I fished and fished the whole night through
I caught a fish and that was you.

Tip a Tap

Tip a tap, tip a tap—listen, can you hear?
Tip a tap, tip a tap—elves are coming near!
Tip tip tip tip tip tip—silverbells are ringing!
Tip tip tip tip tip tip—hear the merry singing!
Tip tap tip tap tip tap—dancing all the day,
Tip tap tip tap tip tap—now they've gone away.

Violets

I know sweet modest violets
  Shining with dew this morn.
  I know the place you come from
  And the way that you were born.
  When God cuts holes in heaven
  The holes that stars peep through.
  He lets the scraps fall down to earth
  Those little scraps are you.

Snowdrops

"Where are the snowdrops?" asked the Sun.
  "Dead," said the Frost, "buried and lost, everyone."
  "Oh no!" said the Sun, "They did not die,
  Asleep they lie and I will wake them,
  Up to the light
  All dressed in white everyone!"

Snow

Snow, snow, snow
  Snow beneath my toe
  Snow, snow I see
  Right up to my knee
  Snow is lying all around
  On the trees and on the ground;
  Snow upon the flower bed
  Snow upon the garden shed
  Oh, how I love the snow!
  Snow beneath my toes
  Right up to my nose
  But now into the house I'll go
  To hide away from all the snow.

The Hazelmouse

One little Hazelmouse
　Sitting in her hazelhouse
　In her home and she will not stay
　Takes a journey far away.
　Once hush, to hazelbush!

One gray housemouse
Came to little Hazelmouse:
"Dearest Hazelmouse I pray,
Take me with you on your way."
Once hush, twice hush, to hazelbush!

One brown fieldmouse
Came to little Hazelmouse:
"Dearest Hazelmouse I pray,
Take me with you on your way."
Once hush, twice hush, three times hush, to hazelbush!

The Shepherd Boy

Here comes the shepherd limping leg
　Who has a sore and painful leg.
　Now to the doctor he must go,
　His poor and limping leg to show!
　"I'll heal your limping leg for you,
　Just let me see, what must we do?
　I'll rub some ointment on for thee
　And bandage it from toe to knee.
　Now, try to step, all firm and strong,
　You are all right, just walk along."
　"Thank you, doctor, I'm all right."
　The shepherd bows and says good night
　And merrily he skips away:
　"My leg is fine, hooray, hooray!"

Circle Games

Autumn Circle

There's a farm on the hilltop in a village nearby,
Where the cocks and the hens on the road cluck and cry,
And the ducklings they quack in the streamlet so fair,
And the sparrows are flapping their wings in the air.
On the bridge stands a boy so stout and so strong,
And he's shouting for joy as a cart comes along.
And the wagon is filled with a load of good hay.
See the horses in front—how they champ, how they neigh!
Right on top of the hay sit our Jack and our Jill,
While the cart sways along to the top of the hill,
And they laugh and make merry and happily sing,
Until bedtime does come and the evening bells ring.

Heigh Ho, Heigh Ho — A. Künstler

Heigh ho, heigh ho, the framer does sow
We sharpen the sickle, we sharpen the scythe
To cut the grain when it is ripe

Come and Let us Reap the Barley

Come and let us reap the barley into sheaves we bind it.
(oats, wheat, corn, or any grain)
Fetch the horses and cart
We're champing, we're champing
We champ and we neigh
To bring in the barley
As well as the hay.
Load up the wagon
Take it home to thresh it there
We're threshing, a-threshing, a-threshing the corn
Just see the grain flying
For none is forlorn.
The little gnome is also threshing. (with small gestures)
We're threshing...
Now gather the grain into the sack,
And load it on the donkey's back. Repeat.
Go my donkey, go.
Take us to the miller's mill
Standing high upon the hill
Go my donkey, go. Repeat

Blow, Wind, Blow

Verse 2

Blow, wind, blow, and go, mill, go,
Up on yonder hill
That the wings may turn around,
Never standing still.
Rushing streamlet turn the wheel
Of the water mill,
Let the miller grind the corn for my sacks to fill.

Bread Baking

Lads and maidens, fair and strong,
To the baker: come along!
Early in the morning hour
Bring the meal and bring the flour, coarse or fine
Corn or wheat makes delicious bread to eat.
But whatever you may bring, don't forget the seasoning:
Put in salt and caraway,
Anise seed or sesame,
Mix it well to make the dough,
Yeast and water make it grow.
Keep it warm and let it rest
For to rise—that is the best.
Now you knead with might and main,
Knead it over and over again
Shape a round loaf, roll or bun,
Stretch a long loaf—easy done.
Stroke them well with water clear,
Gentle hands are welcome here.
In the oven's steady glow
To be baked, the bread must go,
Basking there as in the sun
Getting brown 'til it is done.
Out it comes, all crisp indeed
Fit for any king to eat.

Spring Circle

Tell how the little blackbirds want to eat up the seeds, but the farmer says, "Shoo! Fly away, until I give my wife some grain for the chickens, and then you can share." Then he gives some grain to his wife. The blackbirds come back and peck, and all the chickens come and peck the grain: "Peck-peck-peck" etc. Suddenly the big brown hen starts flapping her wings and clucking:

Cluck, Cluck, Cluck

> *Cluck, cluck, cluck, nay!*
> *An egg I have laid!*
> *Cluck, cluck, cluck, nay!*
> *An egg I have laid!*
>
> *The chicken makes a cluck, cluck, cluck,*
> *A terrible loud sound;*
> *The farmer's wife knows what to do*
> *The egg is quickly found.*

Then all at once the little white hen starts, etc.

And the black hen, the checkered hen, and the red hen...

Now the farmer's wife lets some of the hens sit on the eggs and keep them warm with their wings, and brood on them until you can hear a tiny noise—peck! Little yellow chicks start pecking little grains with their tiny beaks—peck, peck, peck, peck. And the big cock calls, "Cock-a-doodle-do!"

On Palm Sunday, the village children come with branches of the willow tree chanting a sing-song:

Pussy Pussy Willow

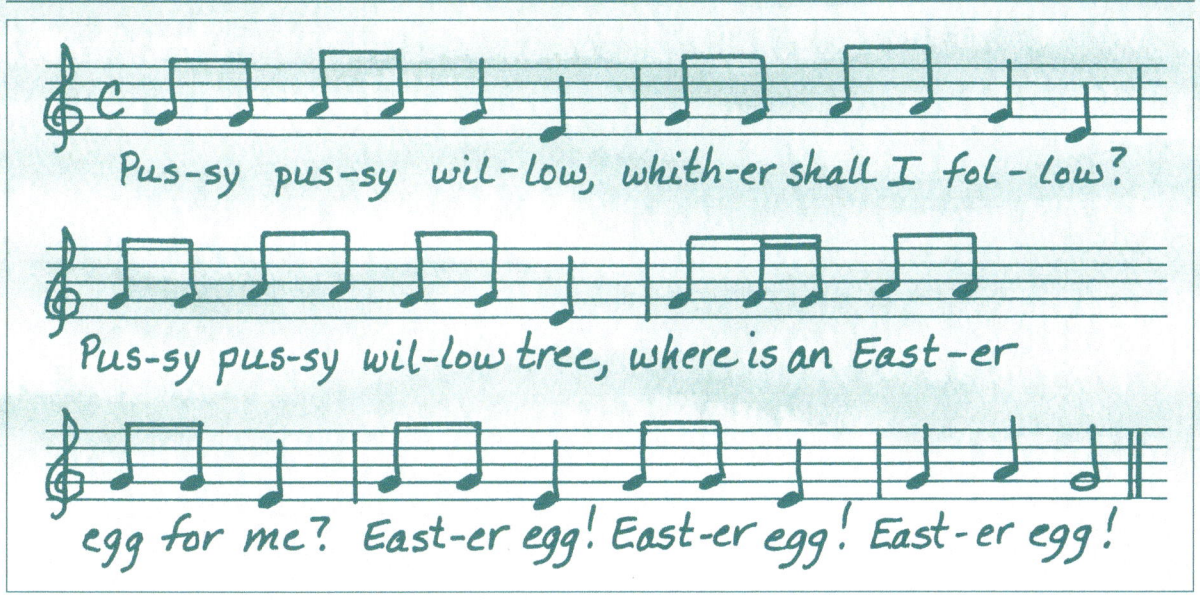

*Pussy Pussy willow
Everyone must follow
Pussy Pussy willow tree
Have you got an egg for me?
Is the farmer's wife at home, is she in?
If you have an egg to spare,
Please put it in our basket here.
Easter egg, Easter egg, an Easter egg!*

—Traditional

Then the farmer's wife brings the other eggs to the rabbit waiting in the meadow.

*By the bushes, on the green,
Easter Rabbit can be seen,
With shining paints—red, yellow, blue
To paint an Easter egg for you!*

He dips the brush deep into the paint. There's a red egg! Then he washes the brush in a little stream and swishes the brush through the air to get all the drops of water out of it. He dips it in the blue, etc.

The Easter Rabbit hops and skips away to find a place for every egg. He hops and hides them everywhere, by the bush and tree and flowers fair. Now come, dear children, come along, to find the eggs and sing a song.

Foxglove: A Circle Game for Midsummer
by Bronja Zahlingen

This circle game is based on an Irish legend about Foxglove, who has a humped back and who helps the fairies at Midsummer and is helped by them in turn. There are country folk, fairies and Foxglove, who can be played by the second teacher.

Ring bell and come out dancing and singing:

We Country Folk Are Happy   Old English tune

Except for little Foxglove
Alas, alas, alack!
Who ever from his childhood
Has had a crooked back.

He loves the herbs and flowers
Just see him walk along
Upon his cap a foxglove
Upon his lips a song.

Spoken:

> *But some people are unkind,*
> *Are not good of heart and mind*
> *When they see him on the way point their fingers, and they say,*
> *"He's a wizard, well he knows*
> *Where every herb and flower grows;*
> *Weaves baskets of rushes*
> *To you to be sold*
> *But witchcraft magic they surely must hold."*
> *"No, no, no, that is not true*
> *Foxglove is as good as you;*
> *Working hard from morn to night*
> *Patiently he bears his plight.*
> *Carries baskets up to town*
> *Over elfin hill,*
> *Now to rest a little while*
> *See him sitting still.*
> *Goes around area indicated as fairy hill.*
>
> *And as the moon is rising*
> *Sweet music he can hear*
> *Can that be fairies singing*
> *In silver light so clear?*

Silver Ferry Glide Away

Spoken:

> *Little Foxglove looks around*
> *In the bushes, on the ground.*
> *No, there's nothing to be seen*
> *"I suppose it was a dream!"*

Repeat **Silver Ferry Glide Away.**

Foxglove speaks:

> "There again like bells that ring
> Hear the fairies sweetly sing."

Repeat *Silver Ferry Glide Away*.

> "Hark! Again the fairies' song,
> But it is not very long
> Half a tune will never do,
> I'll add another rhyme for you."

Repeat *Silver Ferry Glide Away*.

Fairies speak:

> "Foxglove, Foxglove, Foxglove dear
> What a lovely song we hear!
> Come, you fairies on the green
> Come a-dancing, come be seen. "

Repeat *Silver Ferry Glide Away*.

> "Show yourself now, little man,
> Our master singer,
> Show your face and turn around,
> Lovely music bringer.
>
> "Oh, oh, woe, alas, alack!
> What a poor and crooked back.
> Who made such a lovely song
> Should be beautiful and strong."

Sung to *We Country Folk are Happy*:

> We fairies can be helpful
> In high Midsummer night
> Fall off you nasty hunchback
> Grow straight and stand upright!
> Oh joy, Oh joy, dear Foxglove,
> How tall you are and free.

Repeat several times.

Look up into the heavens,
The lovely light to see.
Now join our hands, dear Foxglove,
Come join our circle gay
For here we go a-dancing
All on Midsummer Day!

Repeat first verse.

Birthday Game

There was a little rabbit once
With ears so long and eyes so kind
And a bushy, tiny tail behind
And as his birthday is today
The animals all come along
To greet their friend with cheers and song.

A lambkin white, the gentle deer,
The big brown bear, the mouse so small,
The stag with antlers strong and tall.
The squirrel jumps from tree to tree
While in their nest
The birds do sing.
And all go dancing in a ring
Fidirullalla, Fidirullalla, Fidirullalla.

All dance. Teacher may clap hands behind, over her head, make tiny claps with her fingers, and so on.

Stories

Little Grandmother Evergreen
A German fairy tale
Translated by Bronja Zahlingen

Once upon a time, there was a mother who had two children. One day, when she did not feel very well, she longed for some fresh berries; so she sent her children off to the woods to pick some berries for her. They went along and picked a basket full.

There came along a little old lady, who was dressed all in green, and she said to the children, "I am very hungry, but I cannot bend down so well anymore, for I am very old. Would you please give me some of your berries?" The children pitied the old woman, so they emptied a whole basketful of berries into her apron, wanting to hurry off to pick some more.

But Granny Evergreen, for that was her name, took them by the hand and said, "I do not need so many, just a few will do for me; take the others home to your mother. Because you have such kind hearts, I will give each of you a flower, one yellow and one blue. Look after them well, give them fresh water every morning, and do not quarrel with one another.

The children thanked her and hurried home. No sooner had their mother begun eating the berries than she felt quite well again. That, little Granny Evergreen had done for her. When the children told their mother everything that had happened, she was very grateful to little Granny Evergreen, and was happy that her children had been so kind.

Whenever the children looked at their flowers, which remained fresh and beautiful, they remembered Granny Evergreen's words, "Do not quarrel." One evening, however, they grew very cross with one another. "This is my toy," cried one of them. "Oh no, I want it!" said the other. Thus it went on and on, and they went to bed in anger.

The next morning when they wanted to water their flowers, they had turned all dark and droopy. The children grew very sad and wept many bitter tears. But when the tears fell upon the flowers, the one became bright yellow and the other lovely blue. So the children were very happy and never went to bed in a quarrelsome mood again.

A Garden full of Wonder

An old German nursery rhyme
Translated by Bronja Zahlingen

I'll tell you a story of dear old Aunt Tory. This old aunt, she had a house, and it was a house of wonder. Round this house there was a garden, it was a garden full of wonder. In the garden grew a tree, and it was a tree of wonder. On the tree there was a branch, and it was branch of wonder. On the branch were many twigs, and they all were twigs of wonder. On the twigs were many leaves, and they all were leaves of wonder. Among the leaves there was a nest, and it was a nest of wonder. In the nest there lay an egg, and it was an egg of wonder. From the egg there hatched a bird, and it was a bird of wonder. And this bird had many feathers, lovely feathers full of wonder. Feathers for a little bed, and this was a bed of wonder. Near the bed there stood a table, stood a table full of wonder. On the table lay a book, and it was a book of wonder. In this book, I read a tale, and it was a tale of wonder. Written in this book above, "Share with one and all your love."

The Blue Caterpillar

Originally written in German as *Die Raupe Blau*
Translated by Brigitte Goldmann

One day a blue caterpillar was crawling in the meadow, eating here, eating there, eating leaves just everywhere. He saw a ladybug and said:
"Ladybug, ladybug, how are you sleeping?"
"Moom, moom, moom," he answered.
"Ladybug, ladybug, how are you grumbling?"
"Broom, broom, broom."
"Ladybug, ladybug, how are you laughing?"
"Choom, choom, choom."
"Ladybug, ladybug, how are you singing?"
"Soom, soom, soom."
There came a beautiful red butterfly flying over the flowers.
"Come and play with me," said the caterpillar, "I am lonely here!"
"I have no time to play with you, I fly with my friends to the buttercups."

Lovely Shining Butterfly   L. Henning

"Oh, how silly that I am a caterpillar, I would like to fly with them."
There came a beautiful blue butterfly flying over the flowers. "Come and play."

Repeat **Lovely Shining Butterfly**.

There came a beautiful yellow butterfly. "Come and play."

Repeat **Lovely Shining Butterfly**.

There came a white rabbit skipping over the grass. "Caterpillar come, have a dance with me!"
"Oh, no, this is not the time of dancing, I am much too tired to dance in spring, come back in summer!" The rabbit jumped away. The caterpillar became so tired and unhappy, he didn't want to see, didn't want to hear, and he wrapped himself in a blanket and went to sleep.

Repeat **Lovely Shining Butterfly** (music only).

One day the blanket moved—was the caterpillar coming out again? No, it was the most beautiful butterfly you have ever seen. He unfolded his wings and flew off to his friends, to the buttercups.

Repeat *Lovely Shining Butterfly*.

For a puppet play, we used colored wool for the butterflies, the caterpillar, the rabbit and the ladybug. We used silk for the landscape and some green branches where the butterflies sat down.

Little Flea and Little Louse

This tale from the French, which appears in *Marchen, die wir im Kindergarten Erzahlen*, was collected by Bronja Zahlingen, and translated by Nancy Foster.

One day Little Flea said to Little Louse, "Little Louse, I am going to carry the grain to the mill. Take care that you do not fall into the kettle while I am gone!"

'Ha, ha, ha," laughed Little Louse, "Do not worry, I certainly will not fall into the kettle!"

Then off went Little Flea. Little Louse began to sweep the house, wash the dishes, polish the kettle, and build a fire. There he put the kettle of soup. Little Louse was so tired from all this work that he went out into the garden and lay down under a rosebush to rest. Soon he was sound asleep.

After a while, Little Flea came home. When he saw the door open, he was terribly frightened. "Little Louse, Little Louse, where are you?" he cried. But there was no answer, because Little Louse was fast asleep under the rosebush and could not hear him calling.

Little Flea searched here, Little Flea searched there, but no Little Louse did he find. But in the kettle cooked the soup.

"Alas, alas!" lamented Little Flea, "Little Louse has surely fallen into the kettle and burned up! Alas, alas, I will stay here no longer, I am going into the world!" When he had taken a few steps, the table asked, "Little Flea, why are you weeping?"

"Alas, should I not weep? Little Louse has fallen into the kettle and burned up, and I will not stay at home alone." The table said, "If you are going, I will go with you." It lifted its legs and tottered along behind Little Flea.

Now they came past the mixing bowl on the shelf, and it asked, "Little Flea, why are you weeping?"

"Alas, should I not weep? Little Louse has fallen into the kettle and burned up, and I will not stay at home alone, and the table is coming with me." The mixing bowl said, "If the table is going with you, I am not staying here either." It made a jerk, took itself down from the shelf, and clattered along behind the table.

As they came near the door, it asked, "Little Flea, why are you weeping?"

"Alas, should I not weep? Little Louse has fallen into the kettle and burned up, and I will not stay at home alone, and the table and the mixing bowl are coming with me. " The door said, "If the table and the mixing bowl are going with you, I am not staying here either." And the door lifted itself off its hinges and rumbled along behind the mixing bowl.

Then they came to a nut tree, and it asked, "Little Flea, why are you weeping?"

"Alas, should I not weep? Little Louse has fallen into the kettle and burned up, and I will not stay at home alone, and the table and the mixing bowl and the door are coming with me."

And the nut tree rustled, "If the table and the mixing bowl and the door are going with you, I am not staying here either. " It drew its roots up out of the soil and hobbled along behind the door.

So they came together to the rosebush in the garden. Little Louse was just waking up. He stared in surprise as he saw the whole group coming sadly along.

But Little Flea, the table, the mixing bowl, the door, and the nut tree could hardly believe their eyes—there was Little Louse, merry and lively as ever, in the garden!

First Little Louse laughed,

Then Little Flea laughed,
Then the table laughed,
Then the mixing bowl laughed,
Then the door laughed,
Then the nut tree laughed: Ha, ha, ha, ha!
They all went home happily: The nut tree fixed its roots into the soil again, the door sprang onto its hinges, the mixing bowl returned to its shelf, the table placed itself in the middle of the room, Little Flea sat down at it, Little Louse served the soup, and they ate supper together, very pleased.

The Little Madam

Once there was a little Madam who had a pig. One day the little Madam wanted to go to a wedding, and so she said to the pig: "You have to stay home, little Madam wants to go to a wedding!" But the pig did not want to stay home.

So the little Madam went to the dog and said: "Good dog, bite the pig; the pig doesn't want to stay home, and little Madam wants to go to the wedding."

But the dog would not and said: "Pig doesn't do anything to me, so I won't do anything either."
So the little Madam went to the stick and said: "Good stick, beat the dog; the dog doesn't want to bite the pig, the pig doesn't want to stay home, and little Madam wants to go to the wedding."

But the stick would not and said: "Dog doesn't do anything to me, so I won't do anything either."
So the little Madam went to the fire and said: "Good fire, burn the stick; the stick doesn't want to beat the dog, the dog doesn't want to bite the pig, the pig doesn't want to stay home, and little Madam wants to go to the wedding."

But the fire would not and said: "The stick doesn't do anything to me, so I won't do anything either."
So the little Madam went to the water and said: "Good water, quench the fire; the fire doesn't want to burn the stick, the stick doesn't want to beat the dog, the dog doesn't want to bite the pig, the pig doesn't want to stay home, and little Madam wants to go to a wedding."

But the water would not and said: "The fire doesn't do anything to me, so I won't do anything either."
So the little Madam went to an ox and said: "Good ox, drink the water; the water doesn't want to quench the fire, the fire doesn't want to burn the stick, the stick doesn't want to beat the dog, the dog doesn't want to bite the pig, the pig doesn't want to stay home, and little Madam wants to go to the wedding."

But the ox would not and said: "The water doesn't do anything to me, so I won't do anything either."
So little Madam went to the butcher and said: "Good butcher, kill the ox; the ox doesn't want to drink the water, the water doesn't want to quench the fire, the fire doesn't want to burn the stick, the stick doesn't want to beat the dog, the dog doesn't want to bite the pig, the pig doesn't want to stay home, and little Madam wants to go to the wedding."

And the butcher said: "Yes, I'll kill the ox." He went to the ox, but when the ox saw him coming, he said: "Oh, oh, oh, before I shall be killed, I would rather drink the water."
But the water said: "Oh, oh, oh, before I shall be drank, I would rather quench the fire. "
But the fire said: "He, he, he, before I shall be quenched, I would rather burn the stick. "
But the stick said: "Rou, rou, rou, before I shall be burned, I would rather beat the dog."
But the dog said: "Wou, wou, wou, before I shall be beaten, I would rather bite the pig."
But the pig said: "Ou, ou, ou, before I shall be bitten, I would rather stay home."
And so the little Madam went to the wedding.

The Little Castle

Once there was a farmer *who brought jugs to the market on his wagon. He lost one and didn't see it fall off. The jug lay in the meadow.*
Who came along but a little fly, called Buzzing-By and asked: "Whose is this house, this castle dear, who's living here?"
But there's no answer, no one is there, so she flies into the jug and settles down inside.
There is someone knocking and asking:
"Whose is this house, this castle dear, who's living here?"
"I, the fly, called Buzzing-By and who are you?"
"I am the midget, Singing-Clear."
"Come in and settle down inside." So they both live together.
Again there's someone knocking and asking:
"Whose is this house, this castle dear, who's living here?"
"I, the fly, called Buzzing-by."
"I, the midget, Singing-Clear. And who are you?"
"I am the mousie, Knibble-Tooth."
"Come in and settle down inside." Now the three live together.

Again there's someone knocking and asking:
"Whose is this house, this castle dear, who's living here?"
"I, the fly, called Buzzing-By."
"I, the midget, Singing-Clear. "
"I'm the mousie, Knibble-Tooth. And who are you?"
"I am the frog, called Croak-and-Quack."
"Come in and settle down inside." Now the four of them live together.

Again someone is knocking and asking:
"Whose is this house, this castle dear, who's living here?"
"I, the fly, called Buzzing-By."
"I, the midget, Singing-Clear."
"I, the mousie, Knibble-Tooth. "
"I, the frog, called Croak-and-Quack. And who are you?"
"I am the rabbit Fleet-of-Feet."
"Come in and settle down inside." Now they are five.

Again someone is knocking and asking:
"Whose is this house, this castle dear, who's living here?"
"I, the fly, called Buzzing-By."
"I, the midget, Singing-Clear."
"I, the mousie, Knibble-Tooth."
"I, the frog, called Croak-and-Quack."
"I, the rabbit, Fleet-of-Feet. And who are you?"
"I am Mrs. Fox, called Speak-So-Fair."
"Come in and settle down inside." Now there are six living together.

Again someone is knocking and asking:
"Whose is this house, this castle dear, who's living here?"
"I, the fly, called Buzzing-By."
"I, the midget Singing-Clear."
"I, the mousie, Knibble-Tooth."
"I, the frog, called Croak and Quack,"
"I, the rabbit, Fleet-of-Feet. "
"Mrs. Fox, called Speak-So-Fair. And who are you?"
"I'm Wolf, who lurks in deep dark wood, and I could catch you, if I would."
 "Come in and settle down inside."
Now the seven of them live happily together in peace without sorrow.

But there's someone knocking on the jug and asking: "Whose is this house, this castle dear, who's living here?"
"I, the fly, called Buzzing-By."
"I, the midget Singing-Clear."
"I, the mousie, Knibble-Tooth."
"I, the frog, called Croak-and-Quack."
"I, the rabbit, Fleet-of-Feet"
"I, Mrs. Fox, called Speak-So-Fair."
"And I, the Wolf, who lurks in deep, dark wood, and I could catch you, if I would. And who are you?"
"I'm Big-Brown-Bear with paws so strong."
"Come in and settle down inside."

But when the bear touched the jug with his heavy paw, it broke and all the animals ran away:
First, the Big-Brown-Bear with paws so strong,
then the Wolf, who lurks in deep, dark wood, and I could catch you, if I would,
then Mrs. Fox, called Speak-So-Fair,
then the rabbit, Fleet-of-Feet,
then the frog, called Croak-and-Quack,
then the mousie, Knibble-Tooth,
Then the midget, Singing-Clear,
Then the fly, called Buzzing-By, all of them, all of them.

Atty-Atty-Attic

A number of things can be said about this story. I think it is useful to notice that we found at least two endings to it. We are all learning and telling our own story, that of our people, all the time. We cannot always choose whether the endings are to be dark or bright. Perhaps this story with its two endings helps us see that we can choose how dark or bright our own stories are to be. (Used with permission from Canadian Doukhobor traditions.) —B.Z.

There was once a mouse, Muishka Narushka, burrowing mouse, and she had no place to live. So she went down in the field where the stream ran by, and there she found an old forgotten dry horse's skull, white and empty. She went up to it and rapped on it, TOK TOK TOK, saying, "Atty-Atty-Attic, who lives in this attic?" But no one answered, so she moved in and set up house, sweeping the skull every day, and she lived on there in peace.

One day, there came another knock at the skull, TOK, TOK, TOK, and a voice saying, "Atty-Atty-Attic, who lives in this attic?" and she answered, "I, Muishka Narushka. And you, who are you?"
"I? I am Lagushka Kvakushka, Croaking Frog, and I have no place to live!"
"Well, come in, there's room here for you!" So Lagushka Kvagushka moved in and she brought water every day from the stream and did the washing, too, and they lived on and lived well.

And soon there came another knock at the skull, TOK, TOK, TOK, and a voice saying, "Atty-Atty-Attic, who lives in this attic?" and they answered, "I, Muishka Narushka; and I, Lagushka Kvagushka, and you, who are you?"
"I? I am Komar Piskoon, Whining Mosquito, and I have no place to live!"
"Well, come in, there's room here for you!" So Komar Piskoon moved in, and every night he sang the children to sleep with his high-pitched voice, and they lived on and lived well.

And again there came another knock at the skull, TOK, TOK, TOK, and a voice saying, "Atty-Atty-Attic, who lives in this attic?"
"I, Muishka Narushka, and I, Lagushka Kvakushka, and I, Komar Piskoon, and you, who are you?" "I? I am Na Gorya Vertish, mountainside Tail-flicker, the Fox whose tail sweeps his tracks from memory, and I have no place to live!"
"Well, come in, there's room here for you!" So Na Gorya Vertish moved in, and fetched wild game every day, and they lived on and they lived well.

And yet again there came another knock at the skull, TOK, TOK, TOK, and a voice saying, "Atty-Atty-Attic, who lives in this attic?" and they answered, "I, Muishka Narushka, and I, Lagushka Kvakushka, and I, Komar Piskoon, and I, Na Gorya Vertish, and you, who are you?"
"I am Vezde Paskachish, Everywhere Scurrier, a rabbit, and I have no place to live!"
"Well, come in, there's room here for you!" So, Vezde Paskachish moved in, and fetched green food from the field, cabbage and turnips, every day and they lived on and lived well.

And one day, even before the knocking, there came great heavy steps, STOMP, STOMP, STOMP, and the whole skull shook from the knocking, THUMP, THUMP, THUMP and a deep voice bellowed, "Atty-Atty-Attic, who lives in this attic?"

"I, Muishka Narushka, and I, Lagushka Kvakushka, and I, Komar Piskoon, and I, Na Gorya Vertish, and I, Vezde Paskachish, and you, who on earth are you?"
"I am Vas Vsekh Razdozh! Smash Everybody!"

We have two endings to this tale. Here is the first:

And he did it, great Mischa the Bear, with his great heavy foot, he smashed the skull to pieces and that was the end of them.

And here's the other:

"But you are living in peace, so I won't trouble you," said great Mischa the Bear, and he went away and they still live in peace together.

The Mitten
A Norwegian tale
Translated by Karin Kinsey

Once upon a time, in the middle of winter, an old man and his dog went out walking in the woods. And it happened that the old man lost one of his mittens. Later that day, a small mouse came scurrying by. "This shall be my house for tonight," he cried, and he popped into the mitten.

A short while, after a small frog appeared. He stopped outside the mitten and asked, "May I ask who lives here?"
"Littlemouse Whiskers Thick, and who are you?"
"Longlegs Frisky Frog. May I live here, too?"
"Certainly, please come in."

The sun was just settting when a small rabbit came hopping out of the brush. He stopped in front of the mitten and asked, "Who is it that lives here?"
"Littlemouse Whiskers Thick."
"Longlegs Frisky Frog, and who are you?"
"Fur-rabbit Run-so-quick. May I live here, too?"
"Yes, of course."

Now there were three who lived in the mitten, and it began to be quite warm inside. Towards evening, a fox stopped outside and asked, "Who, may I ask, lives here?"
"Littlemouse Whiskers Thick."
"Longlegs Frisky Frog."
"Fur-rabbit Run-so-quick, and who are you?"
"Mother Fox Silver Paws. May I live here, too?"
"Yes, you may."

Now there were four who sat inside peeking out at the snow. Suddenly a large wolf came out of the woods. He stopped in front of the mitten and asked, "Who, may I ask, lives here?"
"Littlemouse Whiskers Thick."
"Longlegs Frisky Frog."
"Fur-rabbit Run-so-quick."
"Mother Fox Silver Paws, and who are you?"
"Grey Wolf Bushy Tail. May I live here, too?"
"All right," they said.

Grey Wolf crept into the mitten. Now there were five animals living there. Later in the evening they heard a loud crashing, and a wild boar stopped just outside. "Who lives here?" he asked impatiently.
"Littlemouse Whiskers Thick."
"Longlegs Frisky Frog."
"Fur-rabbit Run-so-quick."
"Mother Fox Silver Paws."
"Grey Wolf Bushy Tail, and who are you?"
"Wild Boar on the Trail. May I live here, too?"
"Only if you're not too big," they said.
"Don't worry. I'll make myself small enough."

Now there were six inside. They sat so close to one another they could hardly breathe. Suddenly, there was the sound of a branch breaking, and a huge bear came through the trees. "Who lives here?" he boomed.
"Littlemouse Whiskers Thick."
"Longlegs Frisky Frog."
"Fur-rabbit Run-so-quick."
"Mother Fox Silver Paws."
"Grey Wolf Bushy Tail."
"Wild Boar on the Trail, and who are you?"
"Great Growler Brown Bear, May I live here, too?"
"No!" they all cried, "We have no room!"
"Oh, surely you do," replied Great Growler, "just press yourselves together a bit more."

And he crept inside, and there was a great groaning and creaking in all the seams. Now there were seven inside. In the meantime, the old man noticed that he was missing one of his mittens, and he and the dog turned around and went back to look for it. After a time the dog ran on ahead. Suddenly, he saw something moving in the snow, and he began to bark, "Voff! Voff! Voff!"

Then all the animals sprang out of the mitten and vanished in the woods. The old man came and stooped down and picked up the mitten. He put it on. How amazed he was to find it so good and warm after lying a whole night in the snow.

Plays for Puppets and Marionettes

The Giant and the Gnome

This play can be portrayed with knotted cloth dolls, using two extra pieces of fabric to wrap the giant's feet. The children may watch you knotting the characters.

*There was a giant, big and bold,
Whose feet were getting very cold.
He came along to our town
And walked the streets all up and down,
Calling, "Is no one hearing me?
My toes are freezing bitterly!
No single shop that I could tell
Has stockings giant-size to sell."
A little gnome both old and wise,
He gave him very good advice.
He brought two pretty bits of stuff;
The giant thought them good enough.
He wrapped his feet, his pain was eased,
And home he walked, content and pleased.*

The Hungry Cat
Based on a Norwegian tale

The hungry cat can be created in front of the children by using a square of cotton cloth, preferably red. Take two corners on the same side and tie them together into a knot with the ends sticking out. These are the cat's ears. Then put your hand between the two ears, and grasping the cloth, make a fist; this loosely forms the cat's head. Then wrap the remaining cloth around your arm for the body. When you come to the part of the play where the cat says, "But now I'll eat you, for I'm hungry still," take your free hand that is holding the woodcutter, little girl, etc., and slip it under the cloth. Thereby the cat's belly grows

39

bigger and bigger. Be sure that all the figures then remain unseen under the cloth until each one comes out when the goat takes them home. When everyone is home, and you have said, "Good night," you may unknot the hungry cat and lay it over the scene.

A **hungry cat** *is on his way.*
He looks for food,
He looks for prey.
"Now tell me true, and who are you?"

"I'm the man with the ax, the woodcutter good,
A-cutting the trees and chopping the wood.
Good day, Mr. Cat, and how are you?
 You've come a long way. Did you dine well today?"

"Oh, no! Just half an egg and a little stew.
But now I'll eat you, and I'll have my fill,
For I'm hungry still."

A hungry cat is on his way.
 He looks for food, he looks for prey.
"Now tell me true, and who are you?"

"I'm the little girl with the pretty curl,
A-dancing along and singing a song.
Good day, Mr. Cat, and how are you?
You've come a long way. Did you dine well today?"

"Oh, no! Just half an egg and a little stew;
And the man with the ax, the woodcutter good,
A-cutting the trees and chopping the wood.
But now I'll eat you and I'll have my fill,
For I'm hungry still."

A hungry cat is on his way.
He looks for food, he looks for prey.
"Now tell me true, and who are you?"

"I'm the little gnome, living under the stone.
Good day, Mr. Cat, and how are you?
 You've come a long way. Did you dine well today?"

"Oh, no! Just half an egg and a little stew;
And the man with the ax, the woodcutter good,
A-cutting the trees and chopping the wood;
 And the little girl with the pretty curl,

A-dancing along and singing a song.
But now I'll eat you and I'll have my fill,
For I'm hungry still."

A hungry cat is on his way.
He looks for food, he looks for prey.
"Now tell me true, and who are you?"

"I'm the snail, called Oh-so-slow.
I carry my house where'er I go.
Good day, Mr. Cat, and how are you?
You've come a long way. Did you dine well today?"

"Oh, no! Just half an egg and a little stew;
And the man with the ax. the woodcutter good,
A-cutting the trees and chopping the wood;
And the little girl with the pretty curl,
A-dancing along and singing a song;
And the little gnome, living under a stone.
 But now I'll eat you and I'll have my fill,
For I'm hungry still."

A hungry cat is on his way.
He looks for food, he looks for prey.
"Now tell me true, and who are you?"

"I'm the goat, the Capricorn,
With the shaggy coat and the golden horn.
Good day, Mr. Cat, and how are you?
You've come a long way. Did you dine well today?"

"Oh, no! Just half an egg and a little stew;
And the man with the ax, the woodcutter good,
A-cutting the trees and chopping the wood;
And the little girl with the pretty curl,
A-dancing along and singing a song;
And the little gnome, living under a stone;
And the little snail, called Oh-so slow,
Who carries his house where'er he may go.
But now I'll eat you and I'll have my fill,
For I'm hungry still."

"Oh, you greedy cat, that will never do.
With my golden horns I shall finish you."

*Now all came out of the stomach stout.
First, the snail, called Oh-so-slow,
Who carries his house where'er he may go.*

While the snail is creeping slowly along the goat turns his head several times watching.

*Oh, how slowly, oh, how slowly,
Creeps the snail along his track.
Seven days he needs a-creeping
Just for half a yard and back.*

*"Come along, little snail, you are on the right track!
I will take you home and carry you back."*

"Many thanks, Mr. Goat, I'm safely home."

Mr. Goat takes all the others home in turn for which they thank him.

"Now you're safely home, and we say goodnight, May you all sleep well 'til the morning light."

Cat And Mouse

At Acorn Hill Waldorf Kindergarten and Nursery, this was performed with standing dolls for the workers, a felt cow, and knit figures for the cat and mouse. The mouse's tail snapped on and off which was always a delight for children and adults. Translated by Brigitte Goldmann.

Once upon a time, there was a cat and a mouse, who lived together happily. They played and danced and had a good time.

Lyre music.

But one day the cat bit off the mouse's tail. "Oh please, cat, give me back my tail!" begged the mouse.
But the cat said, "No little mouse, I don't want to give back your tail. First, you have to go to the cow and bring me some milk."
So, the mouse skipped and jumped and ran, looked up to the cow and said: "Please, dear cow, can you give me some milk, so I can bring it to the cat, so the cat can give me back my tail?"
But the cow said, "No, little mouse, I don't want to give you some milk. First, you have to go to the farmer to bring me some hay."

So, the mouse skipped and jumped and ran, looked up to the farmer and said, "Please, dear farmer, can you give me some hay, so I can bring the hay to the cow, so the cow can give me some milk, so I can bring the milk to the cat, so the cat can give me back my tail?"
But the farmer said, "No, little mouse, I don't want to give you some hay. First, you have to go to the butcher, to bring me some meat."

So, the mouse skipped and jumped and ran, looked up to the butcher and said, "Please, dear butcher, can you give me some meat, so I can bring the meat to the farmer, so he can give me some hay, so I can bring the hay to the cow, so she can give me some milk, so I can bring the milk to the cat, so the cat can give me back my tail?"

But the butcher said, "No, little mouse, I don't want to give you some meat. First, you have to go to the baker to bring me some bread."

So, the mouse skipped and jumped and ran, looked up to the baker and said, "Please, dear baker, can you give me some bread, so I can bring the bread to the butcher, so he can give me some meat, so I can bring the meat to the farmer, so he can give me some hay, so I can bring the hay to the cow, so she can give me some milk, so I can bring the milk to the cat, so the cat can give me back my tail?"

Now the baker was a good man and said, "Yes, little mouse, I can give you some bread, but you must promise not to nibble at my flour anymore."

And the baker gave some bread to the mouse so she could bring it to the butcher. The butcher gave some meat to the mouse so she could bring it to the farmer. The farmer gave some hay to the mouse so she could give it to the cow. The cow liked the hay and allowed the mouse to milk her: "Strip, strap, stroll, make the bucket full; strip, strap, stroll, make the bucket full." The mouse brought the milk to the cat and the cat liked it very much. Then the cat gave back the tail and the mouse was very glad. They played and danced and had a good time together.

Lyre music.

The Mushroom in the Rain
Adapted from Russian
by teachers at Acorn Hill Waldorf Kindergarten and Nursery

This play was done with simple table puppets. The mushroom was made of silk over unspun wool. The silk rose out of a hole in a piece of wood and each time it "grew," more silk was pulled out of the opening in the wood. As the silk was pulled, the wool fluffed up a bit and the growing mushroom was most effective.

There was an ant who was caught in the rain. "Where can I hide?" he wondered, in vain.
He saw a mushroom peeking out,
He crawled underneath and looked about.
He waited and waited for the rain to stop.
But it rained even harder on the mushroom top.

A wet butterfly fell down nearby.
Crawled up the mushroom, beginning to cry.
"My wings are wet, I cannot fly."
"Come in dear cousin, here you can dry."
The ant moved over, made room for more.
And the rain fell harder than it did before.

A mouse ran up, all drenched to the bone.
"Let me in," she cried, "I am far from home."
"There's hardly room here, but we'll closer come."
Said the butterfly and the ant in one.
They huddled together, made room for the mouse,
While the rain fell harder on their mushroom house.

A sparrow flew down to the forest floor,
Her feathers were dripping, her wings were sore.
"I need to rest 'til the rain has stopped,
I'm battered about from bottom to top."

"Come in, dear cousin," said her friends inside.
"We have more room in the back," they cried.
So, they huddled together, made room for the bird.
Looked out at it raining, not speaking a word.

A rabbit hopped into the clearing nearby.
And seeing the mushroom, "Oh, hide me!" he cried.
"Save me, be quick, a fox chases me."
"Let's bring him inside, a shelter we'll be."
The rabbit was hidden, the old fox sighed.
"Have you seen in the woods a rabbit nearby?"
"You silly fox, how could it be?
Can't you see we have hardly room for three?"
The fox turned his nose, flicked his tail and ran off.
As the little friends huddled 'neath the mushroom top.

Then the clouds went away,
And the sun shone bright
While each little creature came out in the light.
The rabbit hopped out and into the glen,
The bird flew off to her nest again.
The mouse ran off and did not stop,
The butterfly lit on a flower top.
The little ant wondered as he crawled away,
Why was there so much room to stay?
A frog nearby croaked loudly, "So,
Don't you know when it rains the mushrooms grow?"

The Little Boy Who Wanted To Be Carried Along All the Time
Poem by F. Ruckert
Adapted by Suse Konig

A dear little boy, all bonny and gay,
Went out for a walk on a bright, sunny day.
He hopped and he skipped and went dancing along
With a hey! and a ho! and a merry song.
'Til at last his feet were getting all sore,
And he cried out aloud, "I can't walk any more!
I do wish that someone would listen to me,
I wish that someone would carry me!"
And behold—a streamlet, a murmuring brook
Came flowing by, which the little boy took;
Through the waves, through the water the journey did go.
And the little boy said, "I like it so."

But the water was cold, of course, you know,
And he cried aloud, "I don't like it, no!
I do wish that someone would listen to me,
I wish that someone would carry me!"
And then there came a fine little boat,
And he sat down inside, and the boat was afloat.
Along the waves did the little boat go,
And the little boy said, "I like it so!"

But the boat, alas, was narrow and small,
And the little boy was afraid to fall.
So, he cried out loud, "I don't like it, no!"
I do wish that someone would listen to me,
I wish that someone would carry me!"

A snail came along, his fear was eased,
He sat high on its house and was very pleased.
And safe and steady their ride did go,
And the little boy said, "I like it so!"
But the snail was no horse, of course, you know,
He crept along and was terribly slow.
And the little boy cried, "I don't like it, no!
I do wish that someone would listen to me,
I wish that someone would carry me!"

Then a kindly horseman came passing by,
Who seated the boy on his saddle high.
The little boy on horseback sat,

And merrily said, "I do like that!"
But the horse, you know, was galloping fast,
Over stick, over stone, over stiles at last.
That shook the little boy to and fro,
And he cried out loud, "I don't like it, no!
I do wish that someone would listen to me,
I wish that someone would carry me!"

Then a tree picked him up by his curly hair
And lifted him up, right into the air.
And hung him up in his branches high –
But did the little boy then die?
Oh, no—he's dangling still in the tree's green crown,
Come on, little (Johnny), you take him down.

As an alternative, one may use the following ending adapted by Suse Konig:

So, then the horse was turning around
And threw that little boy down to the ground.
The fiery horse now galloped away
While the little boy on the green grass lay.
'Til a shepherd came, very kind and old,
Who was leading his sheep along to the fold. (Repeat as necessary)
Then the dear kind shepherd, good and old,
Took the little boy along to the fold.
And there he slept with the sheep all night.

Little Boy, Now Go to Sleep L. Weinstein

46

*The little boy slept with the sheep all night
'Til the sunshine came and the morning light.
When at last his mother, friendly and mild,
Came walking along, and she found her child.
She led him home like a bird to his nest,
And he said, "With my mother dear, I like it best."*

The Little Light Horse
By Suse Konig

Once upon a time, there was a farmer who lived in a small house together with his wife and their only son, whose name was Jack. One day the farmer said, "It's about time our Jack should have a look at the wide world and find himself a master where he could learn a good job."

Jack liked that well enough; to go out into the world had been his wish for a long time. Quickly, he went into the house with his mother to get his traveling bag ready. His father gave him a gold coin and said, "Keep it well. Should you be in need, it may help you."

Wandering Song   Words: R. Zimmer, translated by B. Zahlinger/Music: A. Künstler

*The humming bee will show and tell
To like my work and do it well.
I learn from heaven high above
To greet the whole wide world with love.*

47

When noon came, he found himself a shady spot and sat down to eat his bread. An old man came out of the forest and said, "I see you are of good cheer, young and strong. Surely you'll be the right one to free the beautiful princess. The great magician keeps her in his castle."

"Oh, this I would gladly try," said Jack. "If only I knew where to find the castle."

"Only the little light horse knows the way, and it can lead you there," said the old man. "Here, near this old oak tree the horse takes off into the forest; if you can call it by its name it will stop, and you can get onto its back. The little light horse will carry you through the magic forest. Hold on tight, don't speak a word and do everything the horse tells you." The old man had disappeared.

"Ho," thought Jack, "just let the horse come. Why do I need to know its name? I am quick and nimble enough to catch it." Jack hid behind the oak tree. The little light horse came along. Jack jumped up to catch it, but it ran away, as fast as the wind, and Jack could but look. "Ah, this is not as easy as I have thought. I suppose I ought to know his name. What might be the name? White horse, I suppose. "

"No, Jack, that is wrong, for shame.

White horse, that is not the name!"

"Well, I suppose then. . .Fast as the Wind!"

"No, Jack, that is wrong, for shame.

Fast as the Wind is not the name!"

Jack lay down under the oak tree. "What might be the right name?" It began to grow dark, and he felt the gold coin in his pocket. "Gold, gold," he said to himself softly. A bright star shone upon his eyes. "Gold. . .gold. . .golden star," he said half in a dream. "Gold Star! I've got it. Yes, I've got it!" All remained silent, and he soon fell asleep.

Sleeping Song Words: R. Zimmer, translated by B. Zahlinger/Music: F. Muche

When he awoke, the sun was up in the sky. He climbed into the oak tree, his heart jumping in his breast for joy like a lamb's tail. There! The little light horse came galloping gaily along. Jack kept very still until it was quite close. Then he called softly, "Gold Star." The horse stood absolutely still and pawed with his hoof. Jack just needed to mount it. Then the little light horse carried him into the magic forest.

Soon it grew quite dark; it rumbled in the trees. "Don't be afraid," said the little light horse. "Don't look around, whatever might be coming along." Jack did just as the little light horse told him. Around him there was a rushing and rumbling growing stronger and stronger. Jack hid his head deeply in the mane of the little light horse. Now there was whistling and swishing; a monster snapped at his feet. But Jack kept still. The little light horse trotted steadily on, and suddenly they stood in front of the magical castle.

"Ah," called the magician, "you've come to get the beautiful princess." He spoke very kindly and said, "Do come in and eat and drink, and I've got a good bed for you as well."
But the little light horse whispered, "Don't do it, don't. Stay with me in the forest."
So the magician turned away angrily. "Ah, such a one are you! I shall ask you a riddle tomorrow, and if you can guess it, the princess shall be yours."
The horse said to Jack, "Go to sleep, for the morning is wiser than the evening. I'll wake you in time." So Jack went to sleep.

Sleeping Song, Verse 2
    God's own world, night and day,
    Angels walk their starry way.

When the sun rose, the little light horse called, "Jack, get up." The magician came. "Now Jack, think hard:
    At night you creep easily in,
    In the morning you jump merrily out,
    Mother Holle shakes it and scatters it about."

When the magician came, Jack called cheerfully, "It's the featherbed!"
"That was too easy," said the magician. "I shall have to make it harder for you.
    Some animals have it upon their back,
    And people have it upon their heads,
    And little girls' mothers braid it into plaits.
Now guess!"

And Jack says, "Please, children, do help me, but softly so the magician can't hear.
    Some animals have it upon their back,
    And people have it upon their heads,
    And little girls' mothers braid it into plaits.
I've got it! Sir Magician, it's the hair!" said Jack.

"Abracadabra, that was too easy still; but wait, this one you cannot guess.
    Two creatures gray, the one is tall,
    The other nimble and quick and small;
    The big one sits by the hole in the wall,
    The little one dares not come out at all.
Now guess!"

And Jack says, "Please, children, do help me, but softly so the magician can't hear.
    Two creatures gray, the one is tall,

The other nimble and quick and small;
The big one sits by the hole in the wall,
The little one dares not come out at all.
It's a cat and a mouse!" cried Jack.

The magician got quite red in the face and shouted, "You think you've got her, but wait until tomorrow. I shall try you again. Abracadabra. Cadarabraba. " Off he went.
"Now Jack," said the little light horse, "go to sleep. I shall keep awake for you."

Sleeping Song, Verse 3
Heaven's light,
Shining bright,
Greets the world with golden light.

In the morning, the little light horse called, "Jack, get up." And there he was all ready.
Then the magician came and said, "Now my clever Jack, look well. I shall show you my dear daughters. Tell me, which is the princess?" He picked up a stone, and five green frogs jumped up.
"Five green froggies hopping about. One is the princess—now Jack find out!"
And the magician turned around like a whirlwind. The little light horse had come up close and whispered into Jack's ear, and he said:
"The one with eyes of gold, so clear,
This is the princess, young and fair!"

The magician cried, "Cadarabraba. Rabadacabra. Not yet. She's not yours yet." He opened a door and let five snow-white doves fly around, and said:
"Five little white birds flying about.
One is the princess—now Jack find out!"

Then the magician cried, " Razebuz lifizli bazi."
The little light horse whispered again and Jack answered:
"The one that flies highest up into the air,
This is the princess, young and fair!"
"Cadarabraba," cried the magician. "Not yet have I lost. Come into the castle." And he led Jack up to a picture of three maidens, one as fair and beautiful as the other, and the magician spoke:
"You see the painted image here
Of three young maidens, lovely and fair
Now tell me Jack,
Where stands your bride,
On the left, in the midst,
Or on the right hand side?"

Jack pondered and pondered and could not decide. Sadly he looked at his little light horse. The horse smiled at him and winked his eyes. The magician approached, and Jack turned around as fast as lightning. "Well," said the magician. "Have you found the princess?"
Jack answered him:

*"Neither the one on the right hand side
Nor the one on the left shall be my bride,
But the one in the midst with the golden hair,
She is the princess young and fair!"*

There came a big thunderclap. The magic castle had vanished. But before the palace gateways stood the most beautiful princess. Jack lifted her to his horse, and they rode home to his father and mother. Then all the people came, and the wedding bells rang. The wedding feast was celebrated, and everyone danced and sang.

Wedding Song   Words: R. Zimmer, translated by B. Zahlinger/Music: F. Muche

1) Vio-lets blue and ro-ses red, now the prin-cess you shall wed. Jing-ling-ding, jing-ling-ding, Sil-ver bells ring jing-a-ling-a-ling.

*Meadowsweet and thistledown,
Our Jack shall wear a crown.
Jing-ling-ding...*

*Be my queen and dance with me,
Ever happy we shall be.
Jing-ling-ding...*

Little Spring Play

Introduction—Lyre music

A. Künstler

The storyteller speaks:

Under boughs with shining blossoms
Blossombride is fast asleep,
   Longing for the prince to find her,
   Waken her from slumber deep.
   And the flowers in the meadow
   Dreaming still deep in the shadow,
   Waiting for the light of day,
   Softly whispering they say:
   I shall be called a primrose,
   I'm daisy, bluebell,
   I am the purple violet.
   I'm snowdrop, and I ring
   My bell to wake the Blossombride
   And call the Prince of Spring.

Sing both verses, with appropriate actions:

Heaven's Gate

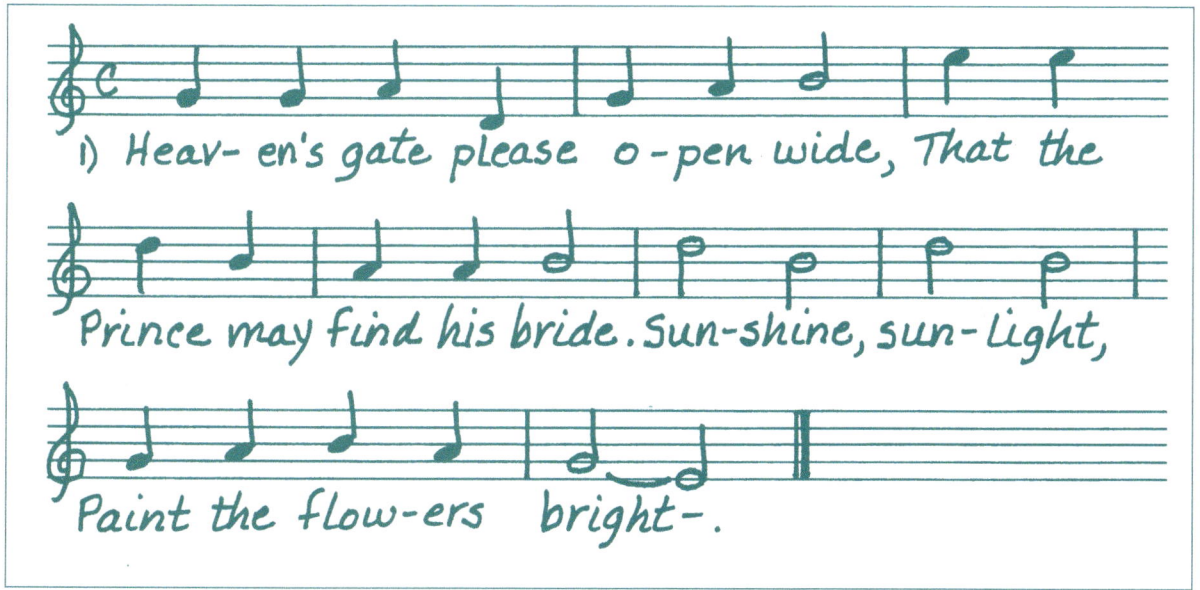

During the second verse, the Prince descends.

Verse 2

> Heaven's gates are open wide
> Sunshine comes to meet his bride.
> Gold light, gold light paints his flowers bright.

Golden Yellow Primrose

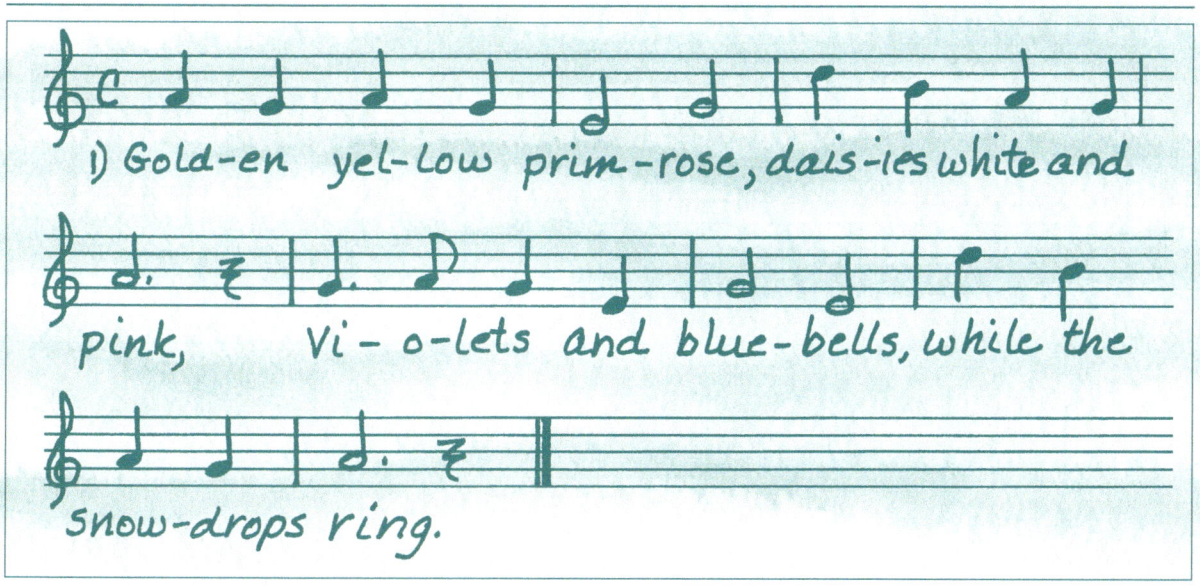

The flowers arise one after the other.

The storyteller speaks:

> *Waken, sleeping Blossombride,*
> *See, the spring is at your side.*
> *Winter's cold has gone away,*
> *Full of sunshine comes the day!*

Blossombride awakens.

Lyre plays d e g a b d e.

Golden Yellow Primrose, Verse 2

> *Flowers are awake now,*
> *All the snowdrops ring,*
> *Let us go a-dancing,*
> *While the children sing.*

Prince dances with Blossombride.

Come Out A-Dancing A. Kunstler

Flowers dance.

A Summer Play for Small Marionettes

Music by Lucie Bittrich
Story taken from H. Rolka

During Introductory Music, the snail creeps across.

The storyteller speaks:

Can you be silent *where green woods grow,*
Where deep in the shade small streamlets flow?
Can you walk without shouting on tip of toe?
Then come! and you'll see how the little folk pass,
Gathering dewdrops from flowers and grass!

Song of the Little Mossy Men   Words: B. Zahlingen/Music: L. Bittrich

Verse 2
   Quickly, quickly, little brother,
   Fill your bucket full of water,
   Save it well for mother earth,
   'Gainst the summer's heat and dearth!

The oldest one speaks:

   I am the oldest with silvery hair,
   I've lived in the forest for many a year. I clearly feel the summer's heat
   When Fireman dances on fiery feet.
   So quickly, dear brothers,
   Do fill up your buckets.

Song of the Little Mossy Men, Verse 2

> *Quickly, quickly, little brother,*
> *Fill your bucket full of water,*
> *Save it well for mother earth,*
> *'Gainst the summer's heat and dearth!*

The storyteller speaks:

> *At last comes the youngest, a wee little man,*
> *He carries and carries and carries again.*
> *For even the tiniest drop will be good*
> *In the heat of the summer for flowers and root.*

Repeat ***Song of the Little Mossy Men***, Verses 1 and 2.

They all sit around the pool. Music as in the beginning. Butterflies fly. [What does this mean?]

The storyteller speaks:

> *If you see a fairy ring on a field of grass,*
> *Very lightly step around, tiptoe as you pass!*

> *Last night fairies frolicked here.*
> *Now they're sleeping, somewhere near.*

Fairies Song, Tune 1

Yellow fairy comes and calls:

Sisters, sisters, do not stay,
Dearest sisters, hide away!
For Fireman's coming on fiery feet
To dry up the grass with the flame of his heat!
Dear sisters away!
For we must not stay!

Fireman's Dance

Fireman speaks:

I am the Fireman,
Burn with my flame I can.
I'll dry up the earth,
I'll dry up the air,
I'll dry up the grass and the flowers fair!

Fairies Song, Tune 2

Song of the Little Mossy Men, Verse 3
(sing twice)

> Quickly, quickly, little brother,
> Pour out every drop of water,
> Fireman, you must not stay,
> We will wash you right away!

Little mossy men speak twice:

> With a swish and a swash
> And away you'll be washed!

Fairies Song, Tune 1, Verse 2
> We thank you, we thank you, green brothers dear!
> You've saved our lives with your water clear!
> Now join in our dancing and join in our play,
> Make merry with us all this summer's day!

Sing several times:

Happy Dance

The children may join in the singing.

Mashenka and the Bear

A Russian tale
Adapted by Bronja Zahlingen

Play music of Mashenka's song.

Once upon a time, by the edge of a forest, there lived an old grandfather and a grandmother. They had one grandchild, a little girl named Mashenka. One day, Mashenka said to her grandparents:

"Grandfather dear, Grandmother dear,
I will no longer tarry here.
Into the forest let me go
Where berries sweet and mushrooms grow!"

So the old people said:

"All right. Just run along, Godspeed, dear child.
Pick all the sweet berries that you like,
On stalks so small, on stalks so tall.
But mind the way, run not too fast,
Come home ere yet the day has passed!"

This Mashenka promised. She said good-bye to her grandparents and went into the forest. She picked sweet berries and mushrooms and all the time found still nicer ones and went further and further into the woods. And when she stopped to look around, she had lost her way. Then she began to run, but she only went deeper and deeper into the forest, until at last she came to a hut that was built of tree trunks. She knocked at the door and said,

"Please let me in, please let me in.
Who liveth here? No one within?
Who liveth in this little house?
No little bird, no little mouse?"

But, as nobody answered, she just went inside. When the evening came, the owner of the house returned. It was a big brown bear, and he said:

"Gruff and grum, who is on my floor?
Now you shall leave me nevermore.
Go light the fire, cook my food,
And bake my bread, all brown and good!"

When he saw the girl, he would not let her go away. So, Mashenka had to stay with the bear and cook for him, light the fire, and make the bread. But she longed to go home again. At last she had a good idea about how to get away from the bear. She got some flour and milk, mixed it, and baked a nice cake. Then she fetched a big basket and said to the bear:

*"Oh dearest bear, I ask you fair,
Please to the village let me go
Just for a visit's sake,
That my old people I may see
And bring them this fine cake."*

But the bear would not let her go and said:

*"Gruff and grum, that cannot be,
The basket pass along to me.
I'll put it by their cottage door,
But you shall leave me nevermore!"*

But that was just what Mashenka wanted. She said:

*"All right, all right, the basket take.
Inside it I shall put the cake,
But mind you do not taste of it,
Nor even do uncover it.
I'll sit right in the oak tree there,
And I shall notice if you dare!
Now look behind the house I pray.
What is the weather like today,
Fair sunshine or cold skies of gray?"*

So the bear went behind the house to see what the weather was like. Mashenka put the cake on her head, jumped into the basket and put the cover on top. When the bear returned there was no Mashenka to be seen, but there stood the basket. He picked it up and started on his way. When he had wandered awhile, he grew tired and hungry, and the cake smelled so sweet that he said:

*"On the tree trunk I will sit.
From the cake I'll taste a bit!"*

But Mashenka in the basket called out:

*"I'm watching you, I'm seeing you,
I notice what you want to do.
Get up, get up, the basket take,
And to the old ones bring the cake."*

The bear was very surprised; he shook his head saying: "Dear me, dear me, how sly is she! She sees me from the great oak tree." He picked up the basket again and went further. The smell of the cake was so s' that having gone so far he thought he might safely have a try again. He said:

"On the tree trunk I will sit.
From the cake I'll taste a bit!"

But Mashenka in the basket called out:

"I'm watching you, I'm seeing you,
I notice what you want to do.
Get up, get up, the basket take,
And to the old ones bring the cake."

The bear wondered: "Oh, she is sly, how she can spy, with her bright eye. She sees me from the tree tops high!" So with a sigh, he heaved up the basket and carried it to the village to the cottage door. He knocked on the door and called:

"Rum bum de dum, unlock the door.
Pick up the basket from the floor!"

But when the dogs of the village heard the bear, they began to bark. They barked so loudly that the bear just placed the basket before the door and ran back to the forest as far as his legs would carry him. When grandfather and grandmother came out of the cottage and saw the basket, they were very surprised and said:

"What might in this fine basket be?
Take off the cover, let us see,
A crisp brown cake for you and me,
And dear Mashenka, safe and free!"

How happy were the old people to have Mashenka back again and how happy was Mashenka to be with her grandparents! They all began to dance and sing!

Mashenka's Song
Adapted from Klein & König

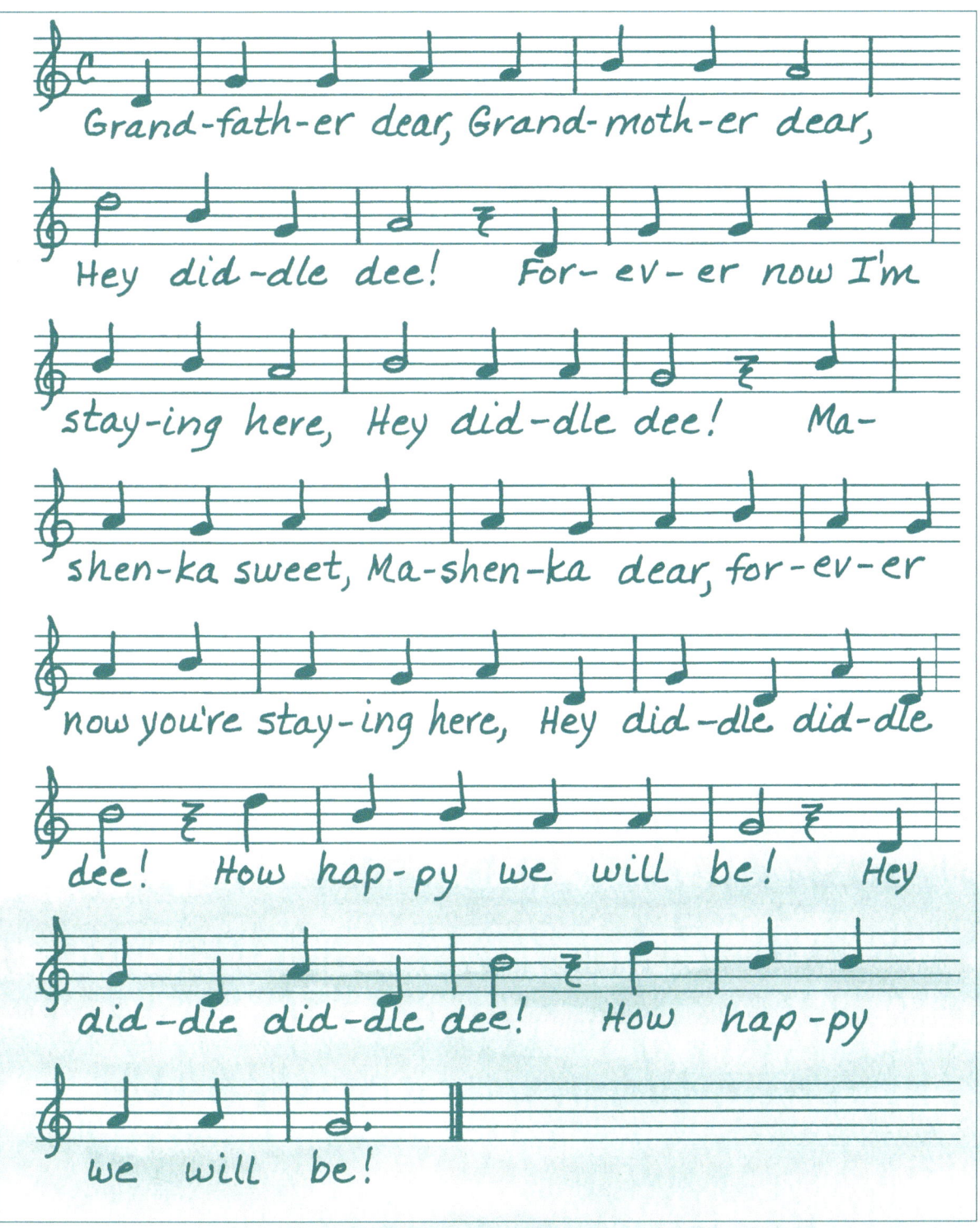

The Swan Geese

A Russian tale

Slightly adapted by Bronja Zahlingen

Once upon a time there lived a father and a mother who had two children, a little girl and a little boy who was still lying in the cradle. One day the parents said to the little girl, "We are going to the town. You stay home and look after your little brother, and we shall bring you a nice silk scarf." This the little girl gladly promised, and her father and mother went away. The little girl stayed with her brother and began to sing and dance around him:

Oh, Happy Day — W. Klein

Thus she went on. She danced outside the cottage as she sang, and as she danced she forgot all about her little brother and ran away into the fields. But as soon as she was gone, the wild swan geese came flying by. They settled down by the cottage, picked up the little baby and carried him away.

When the little girl remembered to come home, she could not find her little brother. She cried bitterly. Then she went out to look for him. As she walked along, she came to an oven that was filled with good brown rye bread.

"Oven," said the little girl, "dear oven, can you tell me where to find my little brother?"

"Eat of my bread first," said the oven.

"Why," said the little girl, "I don't even like fine white bread. Why should I eat your dark bread?"

"Well," said the oven, "then I can't tell you where to look for your little brother." As the oven spoke thus, the little girl went on until she came to a crabapple tree.

"Apple tree, dear apple tree, could you tell me where to find my little brother?"

"Eat of my apples first," said the apple tree.
"Why," said the little girl, "I don't even like the finest fruit. Why should I eat your sour apples?"
"Then I can't tell you where to find your little brother," said the apple tree. As he would not tell her, she ran on 'til she came to a little stream that was all milk and flowed between banks of honey and light jelly.
"Milk stream, little milk stream, could you tell me where to find my little brother?"
"Drink milk," said the little stream, "Eat honey and jelly."
"Why no," said the little girl. "I don't like milk, nor honey, nor jelly."
"Then I can't tell you where to look for your little brother," said the stream, and as it would tell her nothing, she just skipped across it and ran on. She ran until she came to a little hut that stood on chicken legs and behind it there was a spinning wheel. An old Baba Yaga was sitting and spinning and sang:

Spinning Song

"Good evening, old granny," said the little girl. "May I rest a little while? I have come a long way through mud and mire, and my clothes are all wet."

"Sit down and spin," said the Baba Yaga, who went behind the house. A little mouse came along and begged a crumb from the little girl. This she gave gladly, and the little mouse began to speak and said, "Don't cry. Baba Yaga is a witch and would eat you up and your little brother, too. But you have helped me, and now I will help you. Go into the house, take your little brother and run away. I will spin for you meanwhile. " So the little girl went into the house. She found her little brother and carried him away as fast as ever she could. After a little while, the Baba Yaga called out, "Little daughter, what are you doing?"
"I'm spinning," called the mouse, and turned the wheel.

Repeat *Spinning Song*.

Again the old woman called, "Little daughter, what are you doing?" "I'm spinning," called the mouse and turned the wheel.

Repeat **Spinning Song**.

But when Baba Yaga called for the third time, she realized it was the mouse spinning, and she sent off the wild swan geese to fetch the children back. The girl heard their wings flapping and just reached the milk stream.
"Milk stream, dear little milk stream, please hide me. The wild swan geese are after me and want to catch my little brother and me."
"Drink milk and eat honey," said the streamlet. She drank the milk and ate the honey and jelly. The streamlet hid her under its waves. Then the swan geese could not see her, and they flew back.
The little girl ran on, but soon the wild swan geese were approaching for the second time. "Apple tree," she called out.
"Dear apple tree, please hide me. The swan geese are after me and want to catch my little brother and me."
"Eat of my apples," said the apple tree. She ate the sour apples, and the tree hid her under its branches. The wild geese did not find her.
On she ran, but again the wild swan geese came along. "Oven," she called. "Dear oven, please hide me. The wild swan geese are after me and want to catch my little brother and me. "
"Eat of my bread," said the oven. She ate the rye bread, and the oven let her hide inside. Now the wild geese circled round and round over the oven, but when they could not find the children, they flew back to the Baba Yaga and were never seen again.
"Thank you, dear oven," said the little girl, who ran on home with her little brother.
Just when she reached the cottage, her father and mother returned from the town. How happy they were to see their daughter and the little brother safely at home. They gave her a little scarf, and they danced happily together.

Repeat **Oh, Happy Day**.

The Snowmaiden
A Russian tale adapted by Bronja Zahlingen

Once upon a time, in the faraway land of Russia, *there lived an old man and his wife in a cottage near the forest. They had horses and cows, geese and ducks, cats and dogs, and many, many chickens. But they had no children. "Ah," they said, "in all the other houses there is such a row and a noise and a chatter going on, and laughing, with all those children. Only in our house it is so still. If only we had a little daughter, too."*

One day in winter, when the snow had fallen and was lying thick on the ground, the children were playing and snowballing, building snowmen and even a Baba Yaga of snow (a snow witch, you know). The old man and the old woman said to one another, "How would it be if we went out into the yard and made ourselves a little maiden of snow? Maybe the good God would help us and make her alive! Then we should have a little daughter, too. Who can tell?"

No sooner said than done. One evening, when the moon was shining brightly, the old man and the old woman went out into the yard together. Carefully they gathered up the snow, gently they rolled and formed a little head, and arms and feet, and lo and behold—there stood a lovely little maiden made of snow. Her lips and eyes were tightly closed. "Ah," called the old man and the old woman, "You shall be our little daughter, our little white dove. Why don't you look at us? Speak to your good father! Laugh to your little mother!"

And the good God heard the old people. The Snowmaiden opened her eyes. She began to laugh. That was like the little silver bells ringing. She began to dance and sing.

Snowmaiden Song   L. Bittrich

Verse 2

See me dancing fast and faster,
Wind shall be my dancing master,
Up and down and round I go,
Little daughter of the snow.

Verse 3

Jingle bells with merry ringing,
On a sled I'll ride a-singing,
Skating o'er the ice I'll go,
Little daughter of the snow.

Verse 4

But should your love not be true,
I'll no longer stay with you,
Back to heaven I must go,
Little daughter of the snow.

"We do love you," said the old people. "You shall be our little daughter, our white dove. Do stay with us." And they picked her up and carried her into the house.

"Not too warm, not too warm!" cried the Snowmaiden when they came near the fire. She sat down on a little bench near the window. Now she wanted something to eat—ice porridge! That was very easy to prepare. You just had to put a bit of ice into a wooden bowl, and crunch it up into little tiny bits. That she liked very much. Then she was supposed to go to bed, but she cried, "No, no! I'm a little Snowmaiden. I don't go to sleep just yet! I shall dance all night in the yard, and tomorrow I shall play with the children in the street. But you go to sleep, and don't worry—I will not run away."

At last the old people went to bed, but every now and then they got up and looked out and saw their little daughter dancing in the moonlight. (Music) In the morning she came to eat her ice porridge, and then she waited outside for the children of the village. And there they came, all the little Sashas and Mashas, and Natashas, the Petrouchkas and Mishiutkas, and whatever their names may be. And they were very glad to see the little daughter of the snow. They surrounded her, they played with her, they went sledding and skating, dancing and singing.

Repeat **Snowmaiden Song**, Verses 1 and 2.

So it went all through the winter. At night she danced by herself, and in the daytime with the children. That was just lovely. But as winter drew to an end, there was not so much snow in the street, and they had to go further away, right into the woods. There they played at hide and seek until evening, and then the children said, "Come on, little Snowmaiden, we must go to bed as our good fathers and mothers have told us to do." But she called, "No, no! I'm not going to sleep yet! I still want to dance at night." And then she ran away. The children waited awhile, and waited and waited, but when she did not return, they went safely home, all the little Sashas, and Mashas, and Natashas, the Petrouchkas and Mishiutkas. They were very good children.

When it grew quite dark, the Snowmaiden came back and looked for her friends. She called out, "Sasha, Masha, Natasha, Petrouchka, Mishiutka!" Nobody answered and nobody came. She climbed up a tree and looked out for them. But still she could see nobody. She began to cry bitterly.

Then trotting through the woods came a big brown bear. He stopped under the tree. "Snowmaiden, why are you weeping?"

"Ai-yi-yi! I'm weeping for my little friends, and I want to go home again to my good father and my dear little mother."

The bear called, "Come down, sit on my back, and I will carry you home."

"No, no!" cried the Snowmaiden. "I'm a little bit afraid of you. You might squash me." So, the bear trotted away again.

Soon after that, there came a gray wolf sneaking through the wood. He stopped under the tree and called, "Snowmaiden, why are you weeping?"

"Ai-yi-yi! I'm weeping for my little friends, and I want to go home again to my good father and my dear little mother."

The wolf called, "Come down, sit on my back, and I will carry you home."

"No, no!" cried the Snowmaiden. "I'm a little bit afraid of you. You might gobble me up." So, the wolf sneaked away again.

Soon after that there came a red fox jumping through the woods. He stopped under the tree and called, "Snowmaiden, why are you weeping?"

"Ai-yi-yi! I'm weeping for my little friends, and I want to go home again to my good father and my dear little mother."

The fox called, "Come down and sit on my back, and I will surely bring you home."

"Yes, yes," called the Snowmaiden. "I am not afraid of you. You will surely bring me home." Carefully, she climbed down from the tree, sat on the fox's back, and he galloped with her through the woods to the hut. There were the old people, and they moaned and they groaned, "Ah, where has she gone, our dear little daughter, our white dove? Where could she be?"

"Here I am," called the Snowmaiden. "The good fox has brought me home, and now you must give him something to eat. He's sure to be hungry."

"Yes, yes," said the old ones. "He shall have a crust of bread."

But the fox replied, "A good crust of bread is not enough for me. I should like a good fat hen! I've brought you home your Snowmaiden!"

"All right," said the old man and the old woman, and they went behind the house. There they began to whisper, and to say, "We have our Snowmaiden again. Yes, we've got her. Shall we give a good fat hen to the fox?" And then they said something else, very quietly, that was not nice at all. They put the good fat hen in a sack, and in another sack they put a big black dog. When they let out the good fat hen, and the dear little fox wanted to catch it, they let out the big black dog. He chased the fox into the forest without anything to eat.

"That was well done," said the old ones. "That was well done. We've got the good fat hen, and we also have our dearest Snowmaiden." But when they came into the house, she had gone quite close to the fire, and there she danced and sang sadly.

Snowmaiden Song, Verse 5
> Ah, you love me not, I see,
> Love a chicken more than me,
> Back to heaven I must go,
> Little daughter of the snow.

"Stay with us! Stay with us, our dear little daughter, our little white dove!" they called. But she rose up into the sky like a little white cloud, and went away. Where has she gone? To Father Frost and Mother Snow, over the stars to the north, where she dances all the summer on the ice. "That was not well done of us. That was not well done," said the old people. "If only she would come back again, then we would know better."

To the great satisfaction of the children, the following ending was added:

And she did come back. The next winter she returned, and she brought with her many little snowmaidens, who danced and sang gaily.

Repeat **Snowmaiden Song**, Verses 1 and 2.

Goldener

Fairy tale from Bechstein
Adapted for a puppet play by B. and H. Zahlingen.
Music by E. Jacobs and W. Klein

Once upon a time, there was a father who had seven sons. The youngest was called Goldener, for he had golden hair. When they went out together, the brothers used to say, "Goldener, you go ahead, for your golden hair is shining so that we will never lose our way." One day, however, they had strayed far behind, and when Goldener looked around he could not see his brothers. He waited and he called, but no answer came; only the cuckoo call could be heard. When he had waited in vain for a while longer, Goldener decided to spend the night in the open air and search for his way and his brothers in the morning. He lay down under a linden tree and soon fell asleep. The night came, and when the silver moon was up in the sky, a shining fairy appeared to him, spinning a golden thread from a silver spindle.

The Finch　　　　　　　　　　　　　　　　　　　　　　　　　　　Jacobs, Klein

The finch all white, the rose of gold, The royal crown the sea does hold. (echo: lyre only)

Early in the morning, Goldener awoke. He felt very cheerful, as if he was sure to find the right way now. He set out on his way, and the fairy song was still resounding in his heart.

Repeat **The Finch**.

Soon he came to a green wood where lovely birds were flying around singing.

Through the Sunshine

From behind the bushes there came a man—he was a bird catcher who used to catch the birds, put them into cages, and carry them to town for sale. He was very surprised by the boy with the golden hair, as he himself had hardly any hair at all growing on his head. Goldener greeted him kindly and asked the way. This the bird catcher could not tell, but he was willing for Goldener to stay with him, help him, and learn from him. So Goldener stayed in the forest; he helped, he watched the birds, and he took great pleasure listening to their song.

Repeat **Through the Sunshine**.

One day the bird catcher said, "You have been with me a long time, let us see now what you can catch. I will wait here, and you hide over there—now try!" The little birds came, they flew around, (play song without words) and they settled down, but Goldener let them all flyaway. One white bird, however, came back and settled down on his hand.
"Look, sir," called Goldener, "This snow white finch has stayed with me."
"Get thee gone with your white finch," cried the bird catcher. "No one has ever seen a white finch. This is black magic; surely the evil one is behind you. Be gone, I don't want to see you any more."
Goldener was very sad. He could not feel any guilt—there was nothing evil in his heart. Sadly he wandered away. The white bird flew ahead of him.

Repeat *The Finch*.

Soon he came to a garden with beautiful flowers blooming in the sunshine. The flowers are blooming like shiny bright eyes, when earth lifts her face, looking up to the skies. There was a gardener at work, digging and hacking away in the earth. What he harvested he brought to market and sold there. "Good evening, sir," said Goldener, "can you perhaps show me the way home?" This the gardener could not do. But he was willing to teach Goldener, keep him, and let him help. So Goldener stayed. He kept the flower beds clean, he watered the flowers and took great pleasure in tending them.

The Flowers are Blooming

One day, the gardener said, "You have been here a long time, let us see what you have learned. Go to the woods and bring me a branch of wild roses. I want to graft it onto this bush." Goldener was very willing to do this, as he had seen some lovely roses on his way. "I wonder what he will bring me," said the gardener. "This fellow with his golden hair seems to have very high aspirations."
"Look, sir," called Goldener, "I have found this beautiful golden rose!"

"Get thee gone with your golden rose," cried the gardener. "No one has ever seen a golden rose growing. This is black magic; surely the evil one is behind you. Be gone, I don't want to see you any more." Goldener was very sad. He did not feel any guilt: no evil was in his heart.

Repeat *The Finch*.

He wandered on until he came to a wide, blue ocean where a golden castle stood high upon the rocks. The fisherman came along in his boat singing:

O'er the Deep Blue Waters

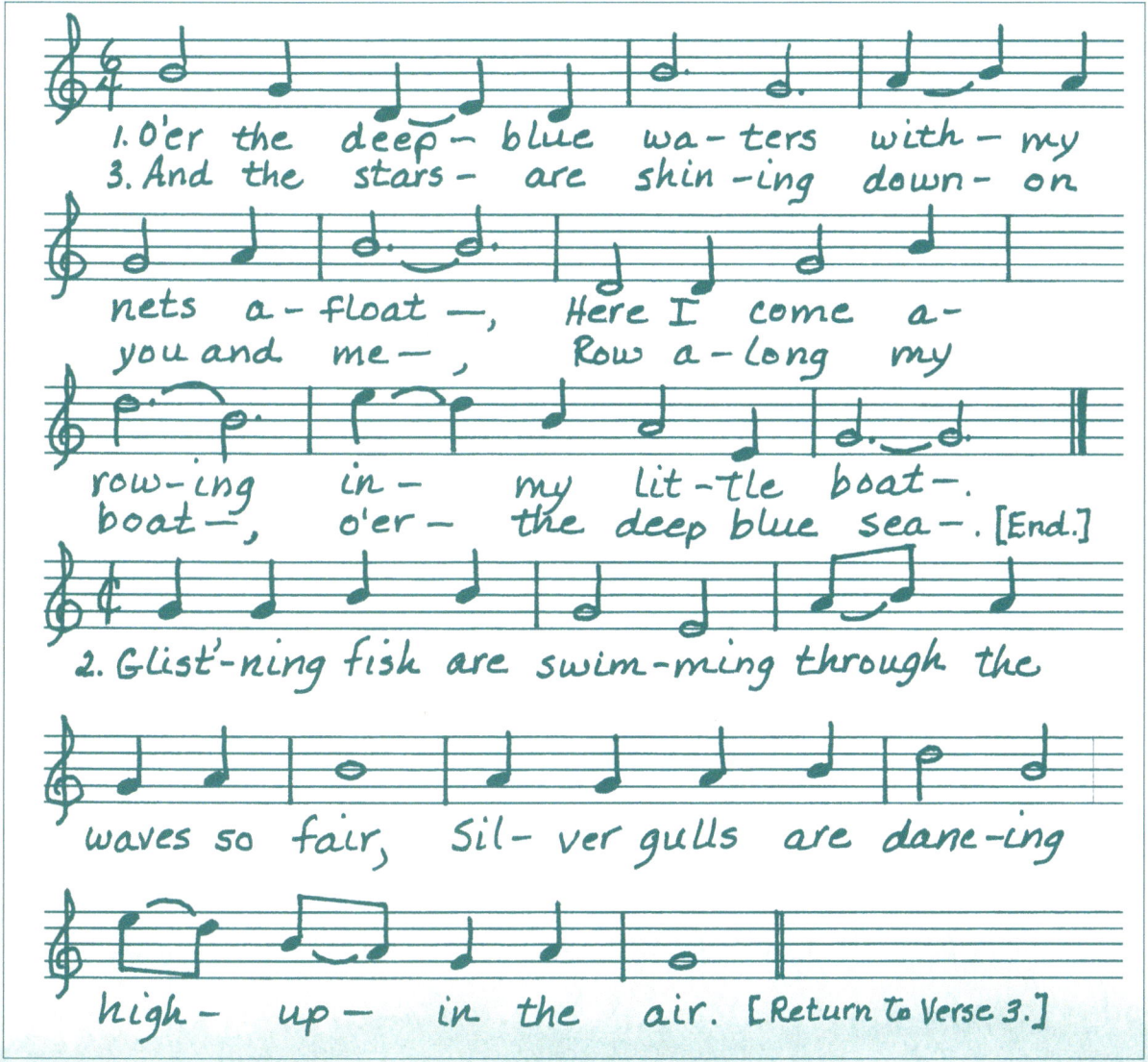

Goldener greeted the old man, saying, "Good evening to you, dear fisherman. Let me get into your boat, and help you draw your nets. They are too heavy for you alone." "That is kind of you, young man," said the fisherman, "that you want to help me, for I am old. Come right in." Goldener stepped into the boat. They rowed out into the waters. The stars were glittering in the sky. And the stars are shining down on you and me, row along my boat, o'er the deep blue sea.

Goldener bent down to draw in the nets, but how frightened he was when he found a golden crown in them. He feared that the fisherman would send him away as the other two had done. But the old man was wise and knew better. He said:

Goldener, Goldener, hail to thee!
Our lord and king you shall now be,
For you have found the golden crown
That was lost in the waters, deep deep down.
Now step to the shore by the castle there
And put the crown on your golden hair.
While from her throne the princess fair
Is coming down the golden stair;
And all the wedding bells shall ring
That you may be our lord and king.
For he that is pure of heart and mind
His dreams of old fulfilled he'll find.

Sung several times over while Goldener and the princess walk up the stairs and sit on the throne.

Repeat **The Finch**.

The Queen Bee
Adapted for marionette play by Brigitte Goldmann

Once upon a time there were two king's sons who started to seek adventures, but they fell into a wild and reckless way of living and could not find their way back home. The third and youngest brother, whom they called the Simpleton, set out to seek his brothers. When at last he found them, they jeered and laughed at him and did not want to take him along. But he went with them. Soon they came to an anthill where the ants were busily running about.

We Little Ants

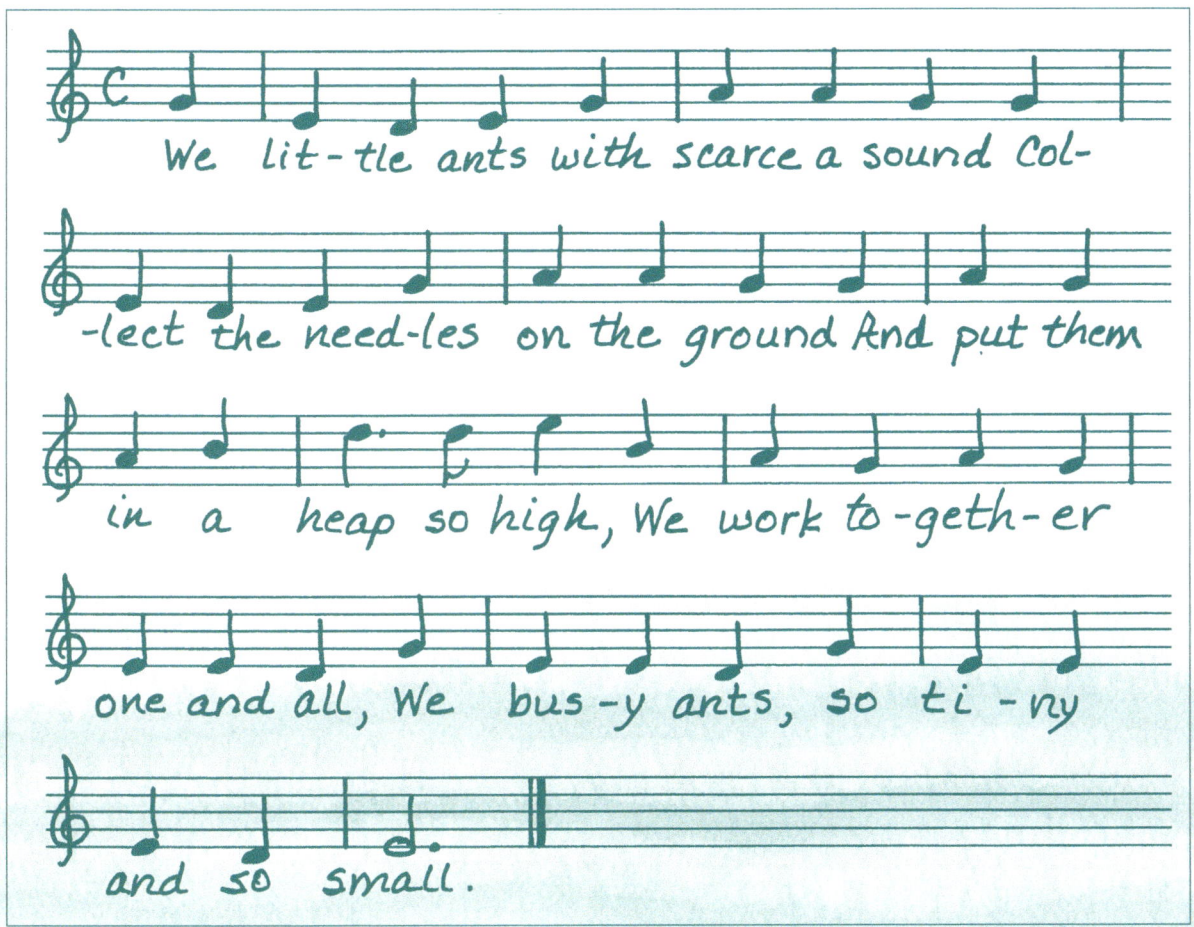

The two elder brothers wanted to stir up the anthill to see the little ants hurrying about in their fright and carrying off their eggs, but the Simpleton jumped in between and said, "Leave the little creatures alone. I will not suffer them to be disturbed."

They went farther until they came to a lake where ducks were swimming about.

Duckling, Duckling

The two elder brothers wanted to catch a couple and cook them, but the Simpleton jumped in between and said, "Leave the creatures alone. I will not suffer them to be killed."

In the woods they came to a tree where the bees had made a nest. They had collected so much honey that it ran down the trunk, and the bees were flying in and out.

Brown and Golden Honeybee

Verse 2

    Gather nectar drop by drop
    From each colored flower top.
    Zumm, zumm, zumm, zumm, zummmm.
    Busy bee ahummm.

Optional Verse
> *Little bee now fly back home*
> *To your golden honeycomb.*
> *Zumm, zumm, zumm, zumm, zummm.*
> *Busy bee ahummm.*

The two elder brothers wanted to make a fire beneath the tree so that the bees might be suffocated by the smoke, and they could get the honey, but the Simpleton jumped in between and said, "Leave the little creatures alone. I will not suffer them to be smoked out."

At last they came to a castle where they found horses of stone in the stables and stones were lying all about, and they could not find a living soul in the whole castle. Then they came to a door and looked through a small window and saw a little gray man sitting in a room. They knocked once, but he did not hear. They knocked twice, he did not stir. When they knocked three times, he got up, undid the locks and came out. He did not speak one word. He gave each of them food to eat and something to drink. Then he led each of them to his own bedchamber.

The next morning the little gray man called the eldest brother and showed him a tablet of stone on which were written three tasks by which the castle could be delivered from its enchantment. The first task was: A thousand pearls of the princess are scattered in the moss. They are to be sought and collected, and if by sunset only one pearl is missing, you are turned into stone. So the eldest brother went out to search for the pearls.

Verse spoken while he searches:
> *Search for pearls, Search for pearls,*
> *I cannot find them all alone, I'll be made of stone.*

By sunset he had only found one hundred pearls. It came to pass as it was written, and he was turned into stone. The next morning the little gray man called the second brother. He showed him the tablet of stone and the three tasks. The second brother set out to look for the pearls.

Verse spoken while he searches:
> *Search for pearls, Search for pearls,*
> *I cannot find them all alone, I'll be made of stone.*

By sunset he had only found two hundred pearls. It came to pass as it was written, and he was turned to stone. The next morning the little gray man called the Simpleton, showed him the tablet of stone and the three tasks. Now the Simpleton set out to look for the pearls in the moss.

Verse spoken while he searches:
> *Search for pearls, Search for pearls,*
> *I cannot find them all alone, I'll be made of stone.*

When he saw he couldn't do it, he became very sad and sat down on a stone to weep. Just then, five thousand ants, the ones whom he had helped, came to gather the pearls for him.

Repeat *We Little Ants*.

By sunset, they had collected all the thousand pearls and not one was missing. The Simpleton thanked them and turned to the second task. The key to the Princesses' sleeping chamber lies deep in the lake.

Spoken verse:
The key must be found
In the lake deep and sound.
The lake is so deep,
I sit down and weep.

The ducks, whose lives he had saved, came swimming, and they dove down and brought up the key from the bottom.

Repeat *Duckling, Duckling*.

They gave him the key, and he thanked them and now could go to the castle and open the chamber of the Princesses. The third task was the most difficult one. He had to choose the youngest and loveliest of the three Princesses. They bore a perfect resemblance to each other. The only difference was that the eldest had eaten a piece of sugar before she went to bed; the second one had eaten a spoonful of syrup; and the third one a spoonful of honey.

Song:
Three Princesses, so young and fine,
How shall I know which can be mine.
They sleep so deep, I have to weep.

Right then the bees, whose lives he had saved, flew in through the window, and they knew where the honey was.

Brown and Golden Honeybee, Verse 2
Brown and golden honeybee,
Pick the youngest one for me.
Zumm, Zumm, Zumm, Zumm, Zummmmmm.
Busy bee ahummmm.

Brown and Golden Honeybee, Verse 3
Brown and golden honeybee,
Choose the youngest one for me.
This one ate the honey treat.
She's the youngest, fair and sweet.

Now the Simpleton knew which one was the youngest, and when he had chosen her, the spell was broken. The Princesses woke up and opened their eyes. Everyone who had been turned into stone came to life again. Even the two brothers woke up and came to the castle. The Simpleton married the youngest and loveliest, and the two brothers received the other two Princesses. They had a big wedding and sang and danced.

Twiggy

A Ukrainian tale, translated by Bronja Zahlingen

Once upon a time, there lived a man and his wife: they were getting old and had no children of their own, so they were sad and thought, "Who will look after us as we grow old, who will bury us when we are ready to die?" The wife said to her husband, "Go along to the forest, my dear, fetch me a little branch, a little twig, make it fine and smooth and shape a cradle for it, too. I will put the little twig in the cradle and rock it and that shall be my joy!"

At first, he didn't want to go, but the wife kept on begging, so in the end he agreed and went off to the woods to cut a little twig and make a cradle for it too. Then the old woman put the little twig in the cradle and sang him a song:

Sleep, My Baby　　　　　　　　　　　　　　　　　　　　　　　　　　　　　L. Weinstein

She cradled it till the evening, and when they got up the next morning, the little twig had come to life and was really a little child. The two old ones were so pleased, and, as the child was so small, they called him Twiggy.

Little Twiggy grew and prospered, and he was so pretty that they never tired of looking at him.
As Twiggy was growing up, he said, "Father dear, will you make me a silver boat and a golden oar, please? I shall go out on the stream and catch some fish and thereby nourish you."

The old father made for him a little silver boat and a golden oar and together they carried it to the riverside. Twiggy got into the boat and went rowing along and singing:

Same melody as **Sleep, My Baby**:

*Rowing in my little boat
On the shining waves afloat,
Catching fish from water clear,
For my parents old and dear.*

When he had caught some fish, he brought them home and then went out rowing again. The old woman used to bring him his food and said, "Listen to me, Twiggy; whenever I call you, come to the bank, but should a stranger call, just keep on rowing."

So the time passed; the old mother cooked the dinner, she carried it to the riverbank and called: "Come to the bank, my Twiggy, dear, come, for dinner time is here."
Twiggy heard her and spoke to his little boat, "Swim, little boat, swim to the bank, for mother has brought my mid-day meal." He rowed to the bank, jumped out of the boat and ate and drank. Then he pushed his little boat into the water again and went on fishing.

One day, however, a snake had heard his mother calling and she slid down to the riverbank and called with a full voice: "Come to the bank, my Twiggy, dear, come, for dinner time is here."

Twiggy lifted his head and listened. "That is not my dear mother's voice; swim, little boat, swim on." He used his golden oar and went rowing in his silver boat.

But the snake went along to the blacksmith and said, "Smith, take a hammer and make my voice as fine as Twiggy's mother's voice!" This the blacksmith did and the snake slid back to the riverbank and called: "Come to the bank, my Twiggy, dear, come, for dinner time is here."
When Twiggy heard the fine voice, he thought it was really his mother. He turned his boat round, calling, "Swim, swim, swim to the bank, my little silver boat, for my mother dear has brought my dinner." So he landed his boat and the snake pulled him out of the boat and wanted to swallow him. But Twiggy was very quick and climbed up into a high tree. The snake tried to gnaw through the stem of the tree and with her sharp teeth gnawed and gnawed. Now the tree was nearly falling over with Twiggy on it! But just then a flock of geese was flying past, and Twiggy called up to them:

Same melody as **Sleep, My Baby**:

*Geese, oh, help me please, I pray,
Quickly carry me away,
Through the storms and through the clouds
Home into my mother's house!*

But the geese only honked, "Let the last one carry you!" and they flew on. Poor Twiggy, he sat there in the tree which might fall over any moment, and that would have been the end of him. But as he looked up, he saw, high up in the air, one goose flying all alone. She must have stayed behind, and could hardly keep up with the others. Twiggy begged once more:

Same melody as *Sleep, My Baby*:

Help me, gentle goose, I pray,
Quickly carry me away,
See the snake I fear and dread
Creeping near to bite me dead.

And lo and behold, the very last goose who had hardly any breath left herself, took him along. He sat on her back, and his heart was beating, for she was flying very low. The snake stretched and wanted to snatch Twiggy, but she could not get hold of him. He was saved. The goose carried him home and seated him on the garden wall, while she herself rested awhile in the yard. Twiggy, on the garden wall, heard everything that was going on inside the house. Mother was baking little cookies; she took them out of the oven and said, "Here, my good old man, one cake for you and one for me."

So Twiggy called from outside, "And what about me?"
"There, someone else wants a cake," the old mother said. She went to the window and whom did she see but her Twiggy, sitting on the garden wall. So they ran outside, took their Twiggy by the hands and were ever so pleased. Then the woman saw the goose in the yard and called out, "What a splendid goose. I will take it and roast it!"
"Oh, no, dear mother, don't do that; rather give her some food, for, but for this goose, I would not be with you now." He told all that had happened, and they gave the goose good food and drink, so she could get back her strength and could fly and follow the others.

As for Twiggy, he lived on with father and mother, went fishing in his silver boat, and never again would he listen to a false voice.

The Miller Boy and the Pussycat

Blow, Wind, Blow Translated by B. Zahlingen/W. Klein & S. König

1) Blow, wind, blow and go, mill, go, up on yon-der hill—, That the wings may turn a-round, ne-ver stand-ing still—, Clip-pet-y clap, clip-pet-y clap, Clip-pet-ty clap, Clip-pet-y clap, Ne-ver stand-ing still—.

Verse 2
*Rushing streamlet turn the wheel of the water mill,
Let the miller grind the corn, for my sacks to fill.*

One day, the old miller said to his three miller boys: "I am old and shall retire soon. Go out and whichever of you brings me home the best horse, to him will I give the mill." The three went out together, and when night came on they arrived at a hollow where they lay down to sleep. The clever brothers waited till the youngest, John, was asleep.

"See. John is asleep now, come, brother, let's go tread softly, tread softly for he must not know."

When the Morning is Coming

Verse 2

And he met with a pussy
All bonny and gay
Come with me,
I will help you,
With me you shall stay.

And if you will serve me all faithful and true
The best of all my horses I shall give to you.

And they came to her castle not a person about,
Only pussy cats dancing and prancing about.

Round and Round We Go

Verse 2

    Round and round we go
    Pussy cats in a row
    Cooking and washing and scrubbing the floor,
    Polishing tables, chairs, and the door.

Verse 3

    Round and round we go
    Pussy cats in a row
    Bring in the salads, soup and the meat
    Pudding and pie, there's plenty to eat.

Verse 4

    Round and round we go
    Pussy cats in a row
    Playing the fiddle, trumpet and drum,
    Now let's go dancing, come, Johnnie, come.

"No, no," replied John" "I cannot dance with a cat! I never learned how!"
"Then take him to bed," said the cat.
Round and round the row off to bed you must go, wash him and brush him and turn out the light, tuck him up
    well now, dear Johnnie, good night!

Short lyre music for the night.

In the morning they woke him up, and he had to work for the cats.

Every Morning in the Sunshine

Text:
>Up and down I swing my chopper silver blade and hand of copper,
>Watch me swing it high and low,
>Look at all the pine logs waiting for my chopper's heavy blow.

Giving back the tools:
>"May I have my little horse now?"
>"Not yet, mow me first my meadow!"

Repeat *Every Morning in the Sunshine*.

Text:
>Cut the grass and mow the meadow, put the hay up in a stack,
>Silver sickle, golden grindstone mind the tools and bring them back.

Giving back the tools:
>"May my little horse I see?"
>"First you build a house for me."

Repeat *Every Morning in the Sunshine*.

Text:
>Build a little house of silver
>Make the roof of silver too.
>John brings back the tools of silver,
>Faithful servant good and true!

Giving back the tools:
> "Now my horses you shall see, twelve are in the house for me!"

Sing to the tune of **Every Morning in the Sunshine**:
> *Seven years now are over,*
> *fare you well John, go home,*
> *And your horses I shall bring it when three days are gone!*

When he arrived home, he found the two other boys had preceded him and each had brought a horse, but the one could not see, because it was blind, the other could not walk, because it had a lame leg behind. "Where is your horse, John?"
"It will follow me in three days." They laughed at him, and, because he was ragged and dirty they made him creep into the goose-house and sleep there.
In the night, in the night, what a miracle so bright, cats ears, cats tails now are gone, let us look for our John.

Sing to the tune of **Every Morning in the Sunshine**:
> *Seven horses bold*
> *Draw a coach of gold,*
> *Many maidens young and fair, the princess with the golden hair.*

Out of the coach stepped the beautiful princess and wanted to see John. They had to fetch him, and she gave him new clothes. He washed himself and put them on, and looked like a prince now. Then the princess desired to see the horses of the other two boys, but the one could not see, because it was blind, the other could not walk, because it had a lame leg behind. Now she called the little horse she had brought.

Galloping music for John's horse.

"The mill is for John," said the old miller, but the princess replied:
> "The mill you can keep, now I take John with me,
> He is not a miller, a king he will be.

Sing to the tune of **Every Morning in the Sunshine**:
> *Seven horses bold...*

They went to the little house which John had built and which had become a noble castle, wherein everything was of gold and silver. They danced at their wedding.

Round and Round We Go

Round and round we go, dancing in a row
John the pussies did redeem
He is king and she is queen.
Round and round we go!

A Midsummer Tale

Once upon a time, there was a little girl who lived with her mother in a small cottage at the end of a village close to the forest. They had a garden where they could grow the vegetables that they needed. Everything else for their livelihood the mother earned by weaving and sewing. The child played in the garden, in fields and forest; she listened to the birds singing, she watched the bees and butterflies as they went from blossom to blossom, and she went skipping across the little stream nearby. Before going to bed, she loved to sit on the doorstep and wait for the sun to go to sleep. One evening, just as the last sunrays fell upon her eyes; a toad jumped out of the green grass and looked at her with its golden eyes as if it wanted to say something. "Toad, green toad," said the little girl, "What do you want?"

Toad, Green Toad — B. Goldmann

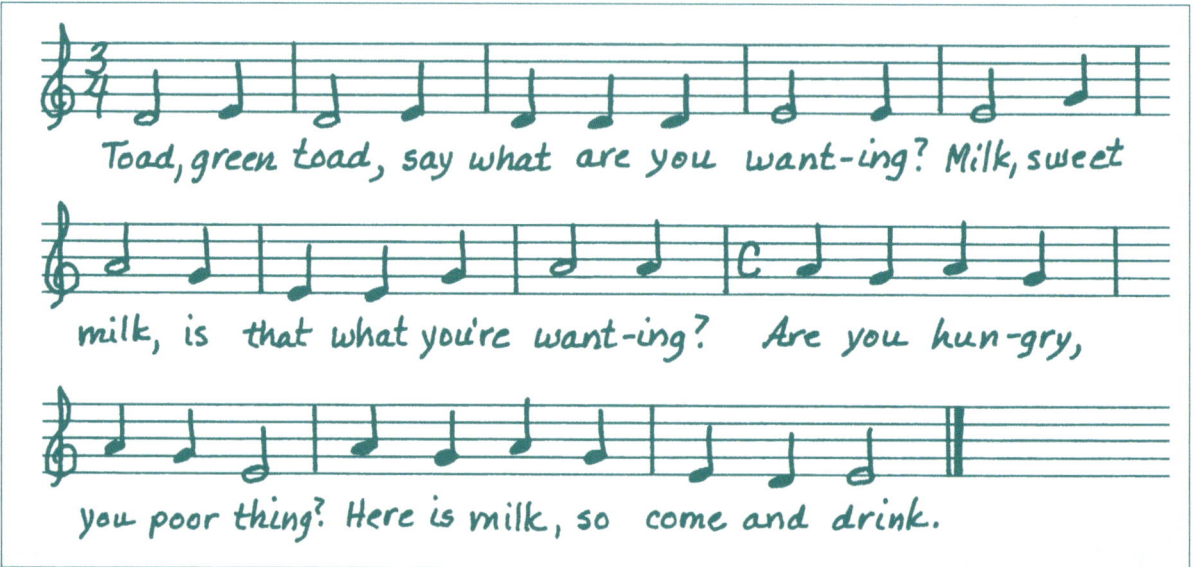

Toad, green toad, say what are you want-ing? Milk, sweet milk, is that what you're want-ing? Are you hun-gry, you poor thing? Here is milk, so come and drink.

Repeat song.

Quickly she went indoors and brought a bowl of milk, which the toad enjoyed very much. From that day on the toad came every evening for milk, and the little girl never forgot to put out the milk.

Once, however, early in summer, the mother fell ill. A sore leg would not heal, and she had to stay in bed now. The girl looked after her as best she could. She also tended the garden, but for weaving and sewing, she was still too young. Instead of that, she began to look after the small children in the village, and, when their mothers went to work, she took them out to play and dance and sing:

On Fields So Green

Verse 2

    Then seven fish in waters clear
    Who heard the children sing
    Went up and down the silver waves
    A-swimming in a ring.

Verse 3

    There seven birds up in the air
    Who heard the merry song
    Spread out their wings and in a ring
    Came flying all along.

Verse 4

    Then seven stars in heaven high
    Were shining overhead
    Now stop your dance and stop your song
    'Tis time you went to bed.

The good little children went home to sleep, and their mothers gave the girl milk and bread and some meal to make a soup. This she brought home to her mother, and however tired she was, she never forgot to leave a bowl of milk on the doorstep for the toad.

Once, it was just on St. John's day, the girl went out to the woods nearby. She wanted to pick some flowers for her mother and also to find sweet berries for her. She took her little basket and went on her way. After a while, she sat down on a mossy stump to eat her lunch. "I should love to share my bread with a gnome," she thought. "Mother says they like it if you share. I wonder whether they live here under rocks and stones and whether they are hiding now. Anyway, I will put a piece of bread down here on the moss, so the gnomes can fetch it."

No sooner had she put the bread down when she heard a fine chuckle and sure enough, there a pointed red cap was to be seen behind some rocks. She jumped up and it vanished, but she could see the gnome running along, and he seemed to beckon to her. She followed to a clearing, why, there were more of them! But suddenly they disappeared again. She followed as they reappeared behind a tree stump. She had to walk through high thistles, and again she saw something red shining under the green fence, and when she bent down, there were lots of red, ripe, sweet strawberries. She picked a basketful for her mother and ate her fill. Then being tired, she sat down and fell asleep. Now she had a strange dream. The toad was sitting in front of her and looking at her out of bright golden eyes. Suddenly she heard it speaking:

"Go look for St. John's wort,
The sun-golden flower,
That bears such a secret
And wonderful power;
If you can but find it
At Midsummer night,
Whatever is ailing
Will soon be put right."

When she woke up it was getting dark, the moon was rising; it was Midsummer night! The toad had disappeared, but she remembered the rhyme quite clearly:

"Go look for St. John's wort,
The sun-golden flower,
That bears such a secret
And wonderful power;
If you can but find it
At Midsummer night,
Whatever is ailing
Will soon be put right."

The girl stood up, took her strawberry basket and began to search for the flower. Glowworms and fireflies flew and lit up her way with their shining lanterns.

Fireflies and Glow-worms B. Goldmann

She followed them to a clearing near some rocks where a waterfall was rushing down.

Water Nymphs

Water nymphs were playing ball with the sparkling pearls of water. The moon shone brighter, again the fireflies and glowworms led her way.

Fairies

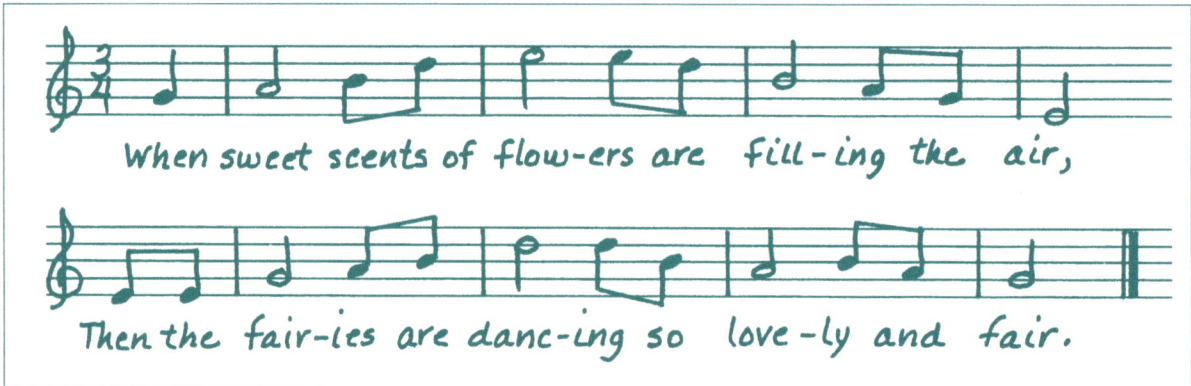

And in the air, light fairies were swaying round and round.

Music and song.

Further along she went following the fireflies and glowworms to the front of a big mountain cave where the toad was sitting on a rock like a guardian.

Music.

Now the cave opened!

Short music.

And there in front of a great Midsummer fire stood a king in a red garment and a golden cloak. Salamander was his name, and upon his head he wore a crown like of flames. He saw the girl, and as the toad was hopping up to her he pointed his golden shining staff towards a green glen. There she went and really, there it grew, St. John's wort, for which she had been looking. Full of joy, she picked a little bunch. "Thank you," she said quite aloud. There was no longer anything to be seen: no fine king, no fairies, no water nymphs. The gnomes had hidden a long time ago already. Only the good toad was looking at her, as if to say, "Go home now with your treasures." She followed the glowworms that flew ahead of her.

Music and song twice.

She had come home.

Music and song several times.

She put the strawberries by the bedside and put some of the St. John's wort on her mother's sore leg. Next morning, the mother felt much better, and within three days, she was perfectly well again. They were so happy and honored the flowers very highly, and the child never forgot to put the bowl of milk on the doorstep for the toad to drink.

Music

The Three Oranges

A fairy tale from Italy
Worked out as a puppet play by Christa Horvat and Bronja Zahlingen

Play introductory music.

Once upon a time, there was a king who had an only son. The boy was happy, carefree and bold. When he grew up, he was to choose himself a bride, but he only wanted to marry a maiden who was not born of a mortal mother. However, there was no such girl to be found in the whole kingdom, and so he decided to go out into the wide world to seek for her.

He set out on his journey, taking nothing with him but three loaves of bread and the blessing of his old father. "When you have found the maiden," said the old king, "come home quickly and tell me, so that we may prepare the wedding feast."

The king's son traveled a long way.

On the Way

Eventually, he came to a crossroad and did not know which way to turn. There on a stone sat an old man who could scarcely see or hear and who begged for alms. The King's son gave him one of his loaves. Then the old man rose and said, "Now I can help you, too. Tell me, what are you seeking?"

The King's son told him of his quest, and the old man said, "You are on the right way. Just go straight ahead, and you will come to a beautiful castle that is guarded by a fierce lion. When he discovers you, the lion will leap upon you, but do not be afraid. Throw a loaf of bread into his jaws, and he will lie down at your feet. Go past him without fear, and the castle gate will open. Go right into the hall, and there on the table you will find three oranges. Open one of them, and a lovely maiden will arise out of it, but be sure to give her a drink of water or she will fade as quickly as she has blossomed." The King's son thanked the old man for his advice and went straight on.

Repeat *On the Way*.

At last, he came to a castle. With a roar, the lion leapt at him, but as soon as he threw the loaf of bread into its jaws, the lion settled quietly at his feet. The king's son went past him without fear, and the gates swung open. He entered the hall and came to the table with the three oranges. Quickly, he opened the first one, and a fair maiden rose out of it, but as he had no water ready, she faded as fast as she had blossomed. Full of impatience, he opened the second orange, and another maiden, even fairer that the first, came forth. But as he again had no water ready, she faded like the first one.

Now there was only one orange left, and the king's son looked around for water, to have some ready before he opened the third orange. Suddenly he saw beside the castle a little lake surrounded by tall poplar trees. There he carried the orange and laid it down on the green grass. When he opened it, a most beautiful maiden, fairer by far than the first two had been, appeared before his eyes. Quickly, he bent down to the water and offered her a drink. Now she became fully alive. Smiling, she came toward him and gave him her hand. Full of joy, they walked together along the lake, and then the king's son said, "Will you wait for me here, my dearest, while I go to tell my father that he may prepare the wedding feast for us?"

"Do not tarry too long," she begged of him. "I am afraid to be here all alone."
"Just sit in the branches of yonder tree, and I will hurry home," he promised.

She sat in the branches of the poplar tree, and the king's son went on his way. The journey, however, was long, and when the evening came he grew so tired that he sat down on a stone and fell asleep.

When it grew dark and the moon came up, an old enchantress came to the lake to do her washing there. Mirrored in the surface of the water was the image of the maiden in the branches. "Come down, fair maiden," she said, "Let me comb your golden hair so that it may shine in the moonlight when your beloved comes to fetch you." Without thinking of any harm, the maiden descended, but as soon as the comb of the old witch touched her hair, she was turned into a white dove who circled high in the air and sang sadly.

Softly Do I Sing B. Goldmann

The old woman climbed up and seated herself in the branches of the poplar tree, and the white dove flew away to the king's son, who slept for a long time. She circled around him and sang her song again.

While He Is Dreaming

The king's son woke up and looked around. The bird was gone, but his heart told him that he must go back to his bride, as she was in danger. When he came to the lake, he was horrified at the odd figure crouching in the branches, but the old woman shouted at him, "Why did you stay away so long? The wind has made my eyes so red, the rain has made my voice so harsh, and the cold has shriveled up my skin! It's your fault! Get me down quickly and take me to your castle and keep me warm!"

The king's son was very sad at the dreadful change that had come upon his lovely bride, but he helped the old woman down, took her by the hand and sadly started with her on his homeward journey.

A white bird circled around them, singing softly. The witch grew very cross with it and screamed, "Chase away that nasty bird! I can't bear its singing!"

But the king's son felt pity for the white dove and said, "It may be hungry." Then he took his last loaf of bread, broke it up into crumbs and strewed them on the ground. At once the little bird settled there to pick them up, and the king's son bent down to stroke its head. Suddenly he felt something hard and pulled out a comb. At this very moment the bird vanished and there stood his bride, alive and beautiful as she had been before. But the old witch was changed into a night bird that flew screeching between the poplar trees and was never seen again.

Then the king's son went home with his bride to his old father.

Ending

The wedding was celebrated with great rejoicing in the castle, and if they have not died, they live there still today.

Repeat **Ending**.

Play of the Four Seasons

This story is not based on a fairy tale. It just presents, like a story, the changing seasons in their particular qualities through the various colors of veils of chiffon or silk. The acting adult carefully spreads them over trees and landscape and removes them again while the spoken word and music please the ear as much as the color pleases the eye. While the bright leaves are swaying and falling, or while the characteristic figure of Mother Holle appears amidst the dancing snowflakes, the child feels the mood of fall and winter as much as he or she experiences the joy of spring with the fluttering butterflies or the bliss of summer with king and queen. The dream-like quality of our little play is akin to the more dreamy consciousness in which the young children naturally live.

The repetition with its slight variations has both a soothing and refreshing effect upon the child's senses, which are much disturbed and overtaxed in our time. In this way, in addition to the joy of perception, a healing quality can be achieved. One might say that here you have, in a special and concentrated form, that which is most inherent in all the single puppet plays: To please the senses and soul and to give plenty of scope for the creative activity of the child's lively imaginative powers.

Instrumental music only: *From the Moon's Bright Silver Light* (page 102).

Once upon a time there was a little girl who lived in a nice cottage with a beautiful garden in front of it. On either side, there grew a young tree, and the child played happily in the garden all the day long and sang:

Heigh Ho, Little Tree L. Henning

Repeat.

The parents, of course, were always very busy, but the little girl never was lonely, for every night when she went to bed, a white bird would come down from heaven and bring her the fairest dreams.

From the Moon's Bright Silver Light   B. Goldmann

1. From the moon's bright sil-ver light, Heav-en sends a- bird all white, While the stars so soft-ly gleam, send-ing you a *hap-py dream.

As the summer came to an end, the bird brought her a dream of the fall. The trees, which had been all bright and green, turned golden yellow and orange. The wind blew the leaves off the branches and called them to a dance.

We Swing and Sway   Pracht

We- swing and sway in sun- shine bright like but-ter-flies in gold-en light, Our gar-ments ra-diant, bright and gay, a-danc-ing we- would go all day-!

Now the wind grew faster still. It shook the trees 'til the leaves whirled around more and more merrily.

Heigh Ho, Whistling and Whirling Pracht

At last the leaves grew tired. They dropped to the ground, which they colored yellow, orange and brown. In the morning, when the little maid woke up, the white bird flew away, but she found everything just as in her dream. How merrily danced the leaves.

Repeat **Heigh Ho, Whistling and Whirling**.

Now the brown leaves had covered the earth all over. Thus it went on all through the fall until one night, when she went to sleep, the bird brought her a dream of wintertime.

From the Moon's Bright Silver Light, Verse 2

*From the moon's bright silver light,
Heaven sends a bird all white,
While the stars so softly gleam,
Sending you a winter dream.*

The trees were all bare, and the first snowflakes fell from the sky. Mother Holle came and shook her bedding and made the feathers fly.

Fly, Little Feathers Pracht

We Are Floating

Mother Holle goes away.

The trees received a white garment, and over the earth the snow spread out a soft white blanket. In the morning, the little maid awoke. The bird had gone. How thrilled she was with the white wonder! Quickly she went into the garden, clapped her hands and turned around together with the snowflakes.

Repeat twice *We Are Floating*.

Thus it went on all through the winter until one evening, when she went to bed, the bird brought her a dream of springtime.

From the Moon's Bright Silver Light, Verse 3

*From the moon's bright silver light,
Heaven sends a bird all white,
While the stars so softly gleam,
Sending you a springtime dream.*

The sun made the snow melt from the trees. It pulled the white blanket off the earth, which now was covered in light green. The green grass shone brightly, and the little trees were covered with blossoms. Soon the first butterflies came fluttering by.

Lovely Shining Butterfly L. Henning

In the morning, the bird flew away. The little maid found everything in the garden just as in the dream. How happily she played with the butterflies, trying to catch them.

Repeat **Lovely Shining Butterfly**.

Thus it went all through the spring, until one evening, when she went to bed, the bird brought her a dream of summertime.

From the Moon's Bright Silver Light, Verse 4
*From the moon's bright silver light,
Heaven sends a bird all white,
While the stars so softly gleam,
Sending you a summer dream.*

The leaves on the trees were a strong green color. The red roses sent their odors and scents, and the sweet apricots were ripening. There came into the garden King Evenfair to meet his queen.

Sleep and Shut Your Eyes   F. Muche

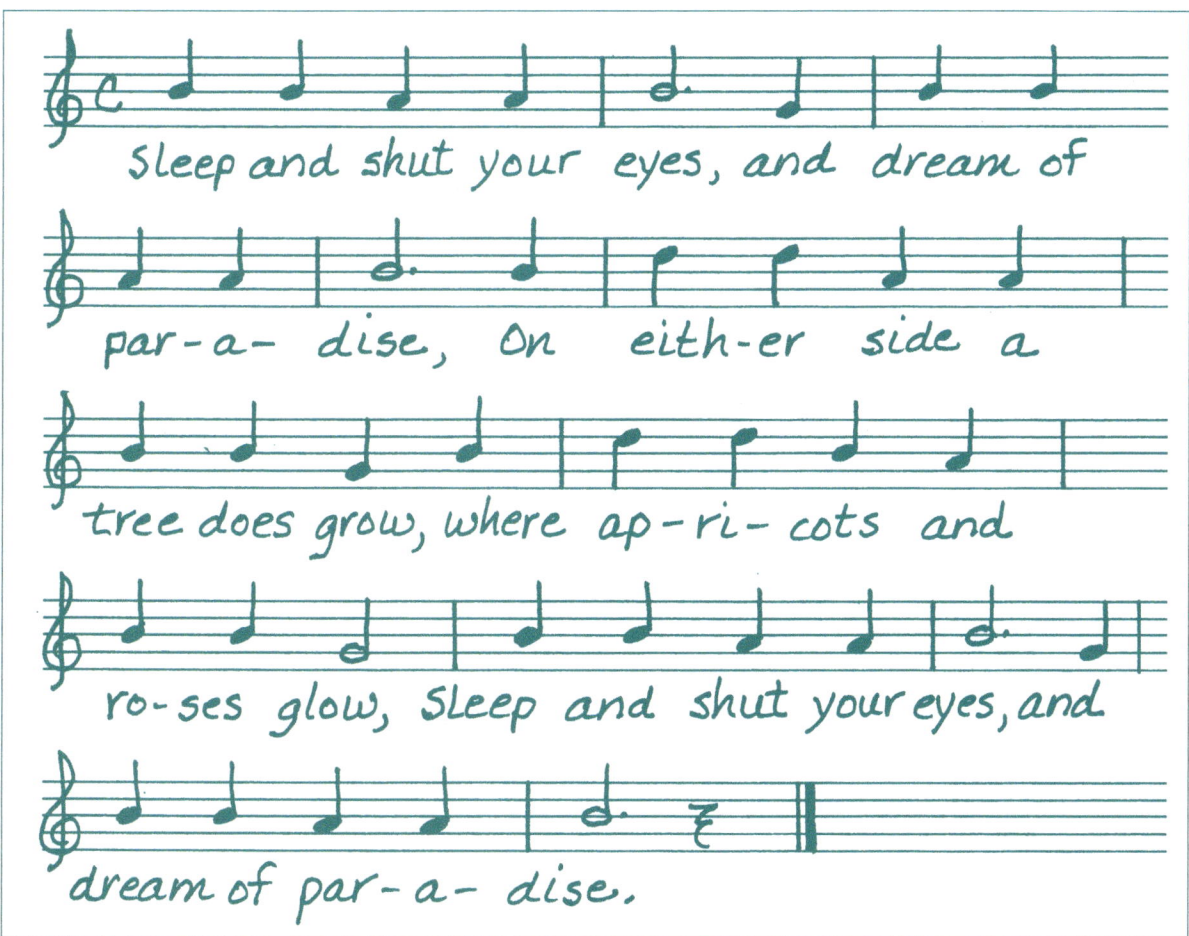

Spoken:
>The king will come in mantle green,
>To pick a rose for his dear queen.
>She lifts her hand that she may bring
>An apricot to her lord and king.
>He breaks it in two that he may share
>The fruit so ripe with his lady fair.
>They taste it and find it very sweet,
>In the midst is a kernel with a seed.
>And the apricot seed which they have found,
>They plant it gently in the ground.
>And the queen prepares a lovely bed;
>She wraps up the seed in a rose petal red.
>A rose petal red, a rose petal red,
>To give the seed a gentle bed.
>To lie in slumber deep and rest
>All cozy like a bird in his nest.

—Christian Morgenstern

Repeat *Sleep and Shut Your Eyes*.

In the morning, when the bird had gone, the little maid went into the garden to the sweet red roses and the juicy apricots. She found the kernel softly bedded in the ground and was very pleased, for she knew very soon a tree would grow out of it, would be growing, blossoming, bearing fruit through fall and winter and spring and summer, year by year.

Repeat *Heigh Ho, Little Tree*.

And after this, she again went peacefully to sleep.

Music as in the beginning.

Directions for Simple Marionettes

Materials needed:

    Medium-weight colored silk, 18" x 18"
    Lighter weight colored silk for veils, capes, etc.
    Cotton fabric, 15" x 15" for underbody
    Unspun wool for stuffing (batts work well for this)
    White or undyed wool for hair (wool roving or other unspun wool works well)
    Sand, pebbles, marbles or metal weights
    Thread for sewing
    Embroidery floss or similar thread for strings
    Gold trim for crowns

Assembling the marionette:

1. Form a round ball of unspun wool for the head, about 2.5" in diameter. Lay the cotton cloth over this, with the center of the cloth at the top of the head and tie off at the neck. Lay the medium-weight silk cloth over the cotton, again with the middle point of the cloth at the top of the head. The silk should hang diagonally so that the points are at the front and back of the marionette. (See Figures A and B.) Cover a pebble or weight with some wool to soften its effect and insert it where the hand should go. Tie off the wrists with thread. Bear in mind that marionettes gesture primarily with their arms, so these may be slightly longer in proportion to the head than would arms on a doll, for instance. The arm can be long enough to allow the hand to reach over the head and touch the opposite shoulder. When the marionette is finished, round off the corners of the silk with scissors. (Figure C.)

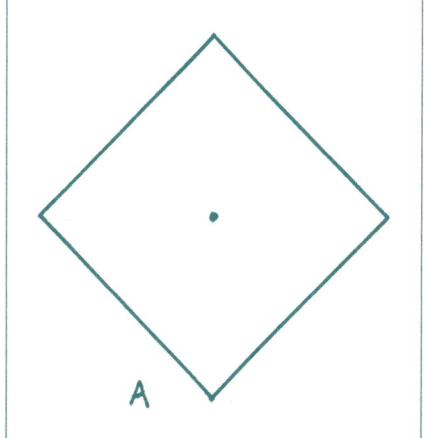

2. If the marionette represents a human figure, in contrast to a fairy or blossom bride, then the under cotton can be formed into a sack that extends about halfway down the length of the marionette's body. The sack should be stuffed with wool and weighted at the bottom with sand or weights. This helps give more substance to the human figures, so that they appear to tread the earth.

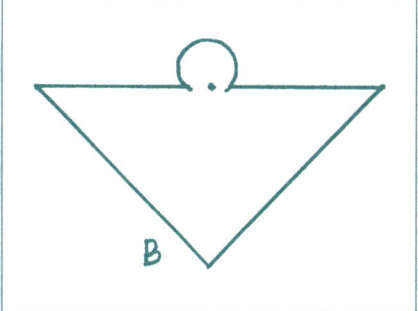

3. Stitch hair to the marionette. Longer roving may be used for female figures or shorter wool may be used. Crowns may be added, as well as veils and capes.

4. Attach strings to the hands and the head. Strings may be about 18 inches long, allowing the marionettes to stand well on the table when you stand behind it. The actual length of the strings will vary depending on the height of the table to be used.

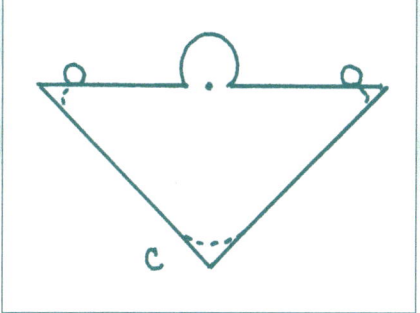

Be sure the head string is centered (it comes up through the head from the neck.) If the thread is too far to one side, the head will always turn, if it's too far to the back or front, the head will bow or gaze upwards.

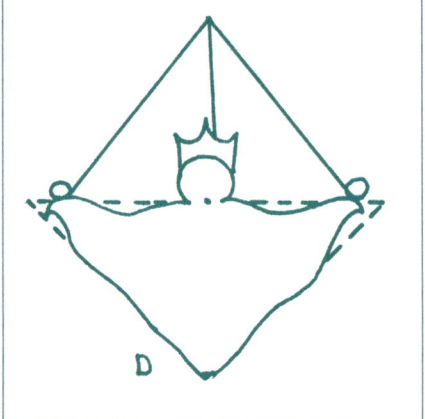

5. Knot the three strings together, or fasten them to a button to facilitate handling. (Figure D.) One more string may be added to the back between the shoulder blades, allowing the marionette to bow.

Nature Tales and Christmas Legends

The Turtle, the Spider and the Wagtail

King Herod sent his soldiers to catch the child Jesus. (He had heard a King had come from heaven and he wanted to be the only King.) But his Godfather came to warn Joseph. Joseph took Mary and
Jesus away on a donkey. Herod saw the footprints of the donkey and said, "We'll find them." But a little wagtail came along behind and wiped out all the footprints.
Joseph, Mary and Jesus came to some water and did not know how to get across. The turtle came and called all his relatives. They made a bridge so that Joseph and his family could cross. Herod's soldiers found them. They said, "Now we'll cross this bridge and find them." But when they got on the bridge, all the turtles swam away and the soldiers got all wet.
Then, finally, Joseph and Mary found a cave for the night. A spider wove his web over the iron of the cave. When the soldiers came, they saw the spider's web. One soldier said, "Oh, no, they are not here because a spider's web is covering it." So Joseph, Mary and Jesus were safe.

How Thyme Became So Sweet Smelling

One hot summer day, in a meadow clearing in a forest, a gentle wind was blowing and all the flowers were swaying as if to say, "It's beautiful today, it's beautiful today."
A little cloud came over the sun. Then a little marguerite said, "Yes, it's very nice here, but just to be standing here in the same place all day is not so nice."
Blue Flower agreed. The Fairy of the Meadow came by. She wore green velvet slippers, a wreath on her head and carried a golden wand. She looked at all the flowers kindly. She was very pleased and even stroked the thistle. She came to the wild marguerite. "I hear you are not content here."
The marguerite replied, "Well, I'm content, but I have to stand here all day. I'd like to be like these clouds."
The Fairy of the Meadow said, "Well, I think you really should stay here but if you want to be like a cloud, I'll let you."
The marguerite cried, "Oh, yes, yes. I want to."

The marguerite was taken by the wind and blown here and there until finally she was torn into little bits.

The Fairy of the Meadow then went to Blue Flower. He also would like to be free like the butterflies. So the Fairy let him go free. Finally, he was eaten by a bird.

When the Fairy of the Meadow came to Little Thyme, he said, "I have no wishes. I want to be just like God made me."

The Fairy of the Meadow smiled at him and said, "That is very nice but I would still like to grant you a wish."

"Well," said Little Thyme, "I would like to have a nice smell. People pass by and never notice me."

The Fairy of the Meadow lifted her gown and a sweet, lovely scent came flowing out. From this time on, the thyme has such a sweet smell people often stop to smell it and some even take it to their kitchen.

The Shepherd in the Feather Bed

Once there was an old shepherd. *He was quite well off. He even had bits of fur to cover himself at night and a feather bed to sleep in to keep warm. Other shepherds came and told about the baby's birth. He heard their excited stories, but the wind was blowing and ice was cracking. He was so warm in his feather bed he did not want to stir. Then, suddenly, he sat up and said, "No. No. No! I am such a strong man lying here under this warm feather bed. And this little baby is lying there only in a piece of cloth."*

He put on his clothes and boots and went off. Now where should he go? He found the stable, went in and gave the little baby his feather bed. The baby sat up, opened his eyes and smiled at him. When this happened the shepherd suddenly felt his heart grow so warm and he felt warm all over. So he did not need his feather bed anymore.

The Christmas Rose

The shepherds went to Bethlehem *to see the child and then went home to tell the others. The daughter of one of the shepherds, Magdalene, wanted to go visit the child. When she arrived in Bethlehem, she found the stable. She was just about to go in when she suddenly remembered that she had no gift and it was his birthday. She began to cry and her tears fell to the ground. She saw a bright light and an angel said, "What is the matter?" Magdalene says, "Oh, I am so sad. I am so poor. I have nothing to give the Child, not even flowers because the ground is covered with snow."*

Then she saw on the spot where her tears fell a little green stem begin to grow up. An then a rose grew on the stem.

How the Daisies Came into the World

Once upon a time, Mother Mary was sitting quietly doing her mending. Her little boy was sitting at her feet. Mother Mary said to him, "You ought to be going outside to play. But it's cold and snowy and there are no flowers out."

But the little boy said, "Don't worry, Mother, I'll sew some flowers."

He picked up the scraps from his mother's mending and sewed some daisies. While he was sewing, he pricked his finger and the tips of the petals were tinged with blood. He ran outside in the snow with his daisies and said, "These flowers should come alive." He placed them down in the snow. The flowers immediately came alive and that is how daisies came into the world.

Vineling, Morning Glory

One hot, sunny day a driver was driving his horse and cart full of big barrels of wine up a very steep hill. The horses were going so slowly that the driver got hot and impatient. He shouted at the horses and used his whip on them. A lady wearing a blue cloak met him on the road. By her side was a little boy. She said, "It's very hot today."

The driver answered, "Yes, my horses won't pull."

The lady said, "Let my little boy sit on your horse—then they will feel the weight so much less."

The driver was surprised, but he let the child sit on one of the horses. The horses suddenly moved on as if they felt no more burden. They went along the road together until they came to the place where they must part. The driver said to the lady, "I'd love to give you a drop of my wine but I have no cup."

But she answers, 'Oh, that's all right. I have a cup." She picked a morning glory from the roadside and used it for the wine. After she drank, the morning glory kept a little pink edge from the wine. The lady blessed the flower and from then on, on hot days in the morning, there is always a little drop of water in the morning glory for thirsty bees and insects.

Mary's Journey Over the Stars
A Story for Advent Garden

Now every day it is getting darker and darker. Children get up in the morning and it is still dark. Mother Mary wants to prepare for the birth of her child. She wanders all over the heavens and then she goes to the Sun, the Moon, and all the stars. She asks them for gifts so that she can weave a garment for her child.

The sun gives her gold, the Moon gives silver and the stars give bits of shining light. Mary starts to weave. But somehow all these shining things won't hold together. She looks down on the earth.

She needs some gold from the earth to hold it together. She sees just what she needs. She takes all the loving deeds of kindness and uses these in her weaving. Then the garment holds together.

St. Nicholas

Saint Nicholas, when he was on the earth, was always a helper of people. Once there was a very poor family living at the edge of the woods in the same town where Saint Nicholas lived. The father was so poor that he finally said to his three daughters, "Even if you have to do something wrong to get money, you must do it."

Saint Nicholas had a servant, Rupert, who heard about these poor girls. He told Saint Nicholas their sad story. Saint Nicholas said, "Rupert, bring me a big fur coat. Bring me a big fur hat. Bring me your big sack."

He put three golden coins in the sack and took a fir branch to carry with him. He went to the girls' house, where they were all tucked up in bed. He pushed open the window and threw in the three golden coins. Now the girls were safe and they did not have to do anything evil. Saint Nicholas went on doing these kind things all his life. Finally he got very tired and was happy to go to heaven. When he got to heaven, God said to him, "What are you doing here? You should be on earth helping people. Well, come on and stay here, but each year one day you must go to earth and help children get ready for Christmas."

footnotes

1   *William Blake*, Kaetha Wolf-Gumpold. (Rudolf Steiner Press: London, 1969).
2   *Truth is Beauty.* Edited by Dorothy Price, (Hallmark Edition: Kansas City, 1967).
3   *The Three Sparrows and Other Nursery Poems*, Christian Morgenstern, translated by Max Knight, Charles Scribner's Sons, New York, 1968.
4   Newly reprinted as *How to Know Higher Worlds.* Anthroposophic Press, (Hudson, NY, 1994)

Sources

Sources of materials for making puppets and marionettes: silks, plant-dyed wool, natural cotton knit fabric, natural dyes, and other materials are contained in *Sources of Supplies, Equipment, Clothing and Books for the Kindergarten and Home*, available through the WECAN Office at 845-352-1690, or online at www.waldorfearlychildhood.org.